Essays

THE SCHOMBURG LIBRARY OF
NINETEENTH-CENTURY BLACK WOMEN WRITERS

General Editor, Henry Louis Gates, Jr.

Titles are listed chronologically; collections that include works published over a span of years are listed according to the publication date of their initial work.

Essays;

Including Biographies and Miscellaneous Pieces, in Prose and Poetry

ANN PLATO

With an Introduction by
KENNY J. WILLIAMS

New York   Oxford
OXFORD UNIVERSITY PRESS
1988

Oxford University Press

Oxford   New York   Toronto
Delhi   Bombay   Calcutta   Madras   Karachi
Petaling Jaya   Singapore   Hong Kong   Tokyo
Nairobi   Dar es Salaam   Cape Town
Melbourne   Auckland

and associated companies in
Beirut   Berlin   Ibadan   Nicosia

Library of Congress Cataloging-in-Publication Data

Plato, Ann.
Essays.
(The Schomburg library of nineteenth-century black
women writers)
1. Afro-Americans—Literary collections.   I. Title.
II. Series.
PS2593.P347   1988   814'.3   87-24745
ISBN 0-19-505247-1
ISBN 0-19-505267-6 (set)

2 4 6 8 10 9 7 5 3 1

Printed in the United States of America
on acid-free paper

The
Schomburg Library
of
Nineteenth-Century
Black Women Writers
is
Dedicated
in Memory
of
PAULINE AUGUSTA COLEMAN GATES

1916–1987

PUBLISHER'S NOTE

FOREWORD
In Her Own Write

Henry Louis Gates, Jr.

One muffled strain in the Silent South, a jarring chord and a vague and uncomprehended cadenza has been and still is the Negro. And of that muffled chord, the one mute and voiceless note has been the sadly expectant Black Woman, ...

The "other side" has not been represented by one who "lives there." And not many can more sensibly realize and more accurately tell the weight and the fret of the "long dull pain" than the open-eyed but hitherto voiceless Black Woman of America.

. . . as our Caucasian barristers are not to blame if they cannot *quite* put themselves in the dark man's place, neither should the dark man be wholly expected fully and adequately to reproduce the exact Voice of the Black Woman.

—ANNA JULIA COOPER, *A Voice From the South* (1892)

The birth of the Afro-American literary tradition occurred in 1773, when Phillis Wheatley published a book of poetry. Despite the fact that her book garnered for her a remarkable amount of attention, Wheatley's journey to the printer had been a most arduous one. Sometime in 1772, a young African girl walked demurely into a room in Boston to undergo an oral examination, the results of which would determine the direction of her life and work. Perhaps she was shocked upon entering the appointed room. For there, perhaps gathered in a semicircle, sat eighteen of Boston's most notable citizens. Among them were John Erving, a prominent Boston merchant; the Reverend Charles Chauncy, pastor of the Tenth Congregational Church; and John Hancock, who would later gain fame for his signature on the Declaration of Independence. At the center of this group was His Excellency, Thomas Hutchinson, governor of Massachusetts, with Andrew Oliver, his lieutenant governor, close by his side.

Why had this august group been assembled? Why had it seen fit to summon this young African girl, scarcely eighteen years old, before it? This group of "the most respectable Characters in *Boston*," as it would later define itself, had assembled to question closely the African adolescent on the slender sheaf of poems that she claimed to have "written by herself." We can only speculate on the nature of the questions posed to the fledgling poet. Perhaps they asked her to identify and explain—for all to hear—exactly who were the Greek and Latin gods and poets alluded to so frequently in her work. Perhaps they asked her to conjugate a verb in Latin or even to translate randomly selected passages from the Latin, which she and her master, John Wheatley, claimed that she "had made some Progress in." Or perhaps they asked her to recite from memory key passages from the texts of John Milton and Alexander Pope, the two poets by whom the African claimed to be most directly influenced. We do not know.

We do know, however, that the African poet's responses were more than sufficient to prompt the eighteen august gentlemen to compose, sign, and publish a two-paragraph "Attestation," an open letter "To the Publick" that prefaces Phillis Wheatley's book and that reads in part:

We whose Names are under-written, do assure the World, that the Poems specified in the following Page, were (as we

verily believe) written by Phillis, a young Negro Girl, who
was but a few Years since, brought an uncultivated Barbarian
from *Africa*, and has ever since been, and now is, under the
Disadvantage of serving as a Slave in a Family in this Town.
She has been examined by some of the best Judges, and is
thought qualified to write them.

So important was this document in securing a publisher for
Wheatley's poems that it forms the signal element in the
prefatory matter preceding her *Poems on Various Subjects, Religious and Moral*, published in London in 1773.

Without the published "Attestation," Wheatley's publisher
claimed, few would believe that an African could possibly
have written poetry all by herself. As the eighteen put the
matter clearly in their letter, "Numbers would be ready to
suspect they were not really the Writings of Phillis." Wheatley and her master, John Wheatley, had attempted to publish
a similar volume in 1772 in Boston, but Boston publishers
had been incredulous. One year later, "Attestation" in hand,
Phillis Wheatley and her master's son, Nathaniel Wheatley,
sailed for England, where they completed arrangements for
the publication of a volume of her poems with the aid of the
Countess of Huntington and the Earl of Dartmouth.

This curious anecdote, surely one of the oddest oral examinations on record, is only a tiny part of a larger, and
even more curious, episode in the Enlightenment. Since the
beginning of the sixteenth century, Europeans had won-
dered aloud whether or not the African "species of men," as
they were most commonly called, *could* ever create formal
literature, could ever master "the arts and sciences." If they
could, the argument ran, then the African variety of humanity was fundamentally related to the European variety. If not,
then it seemed clear that the African was destined by nature

to be a slave. This was the burden shouldered by Phillis Wheatley when she successfully defended herself and the authorship of her book against counterclaims and doubts.

Indeed, with her successful defense, Wheatley launched two traditions at once—the black American literary tradition *and* the black woman's literary tradition. If it is extraordinary that not just one but both of these traditions were founded simultaneously by a black woman—certainly an event unique in the history of literature—it is also ironic that this important fact of common, coterminous literary origins seems to have escaped most scholars.

That the progenitor of the black literary tradition was a woman means, in the most strictly literal sense, that all subsequent black writers have evolved in a matrilinear line of descent, and that each, consciously or unconsciously, has extended and revised a canon whose foundation was the poetry of a black woman. Early black writers seem to have been keenly aware of Wheatley's founding role, even if most of her white reviewers were more concerned with the implications of her race than her gender. Jupiter Hammon, for example, whose 1760 broadside "An Evening Thought. Salvation by Christ, With Penitential Cries" was the first individual poem published by a black American, acknowledged Wheatley's influence by selecting her as the subject of his second broadside, "An Address to Miss Phillis Wheatly [*sic*], Ethiopian Poetess, in Boston," which was published at Hartford in 1778. And George Moses Horton, the second Afro-American to publish a book of poetry in English (1829), brought out in 1838 an edition of his *Poems By A Slave* bound together with Wheatley's work. Indeed, for fifty-six years, between 1773 and 1829, when Horton published *The Hope of Liberty*, Wheatley was the *only* black person to have published a book of imaginative literature in English. So central was this black woman's role in the shaping of the Afro-American literary tradition that, as one historian has maintained, the history of the reception of Phillis Wheatley's poetry *is* the history of Afro-American literary criticism. Well into the nineteenth century, Wheatley and the black literary tradition were the same entity.

But Wheatley is not the only black woman writer who stands as a pioneering figure in Afro-American literature. Just as Wheatley gave birth to the genre of black poetry, Ann Plato was the first Afro-American to publish a book of essays (1841) and Harriet E. Wilson was the first black person to publish a novel in the United States (1859).

Despite this pioneering role of black women in the tradition, however, many of their contributions before this century have been all but lost or unrecognized. As Hortense Spillers observed as recently as 1983,

> With the exception of a handful of autobiographical narratives from the nineteenth century, the black woman's realities are virtually suppressed until the period of the Harlem Renaissance and later. Essentially the black woman as artist, as intellectual spokesperson for her own cultural apprenticeship, has not existed before, for anyone. At the source of [their] own symbol-making task, [the community of black women writers] confronts, therefore, a tradition of work that is quite recent, its continuities, broken and sporadic.

Until now, it has been extraordinarily difficult to establish the formal connections between early black women's writing and that of the present, precisely because our knowledge of their work has been broken and sporadic. Phillis Wheatley, for example, while certainly the most reprinted and discussed poet in the tradition, is also one of the least understood. Ann Plato's seminal work, *Essays* (which includes biographies and poems), has not been reprinted since it was published a century and a half ago. And Harriet Wilson's *Our Nig*, her compelling novel of a black woman's expanding consciousness in a racist Northern antebellum environment, never received even *one* review or comment at a time when virtually *all* works written by black people were heralded by abolitionists as salient arguments against the existence of human slavery. Many of the books reprinted in this set experienced a similar fate, the most dreadful fate for an author: that of being ignored then relegated to the obscurity of the rare book section of a university library. We can only wonder how many other texts in the black woman's tradition have been lost to this generation of readers or remain unclassified or uncatalogued and, hence, unread.

This was not always so, however. Black women writers dominated the final decade of the nineteenth century, perhaps spurred to publish by an 1886 essay entitled "The Coming American Novelist," which was published in *Lippincott's Monthly Magazine* and written by "A Lady From Philadelphia." This pseudonymous essay argued that the "Great American Novel" would be written by a black person. Her argument is so curious that it deserves to be repeated:

> When we come to formulate our demands of the Coming American Novelist, we will agree that he must be native-born. His ancestors may come from where they will, but we must give him a birthplace and have the raising of him. Still, the longer his family has been here the better he will represent us. Suppose he should have no country but ours, no traditions but those he has learned here, no longings apart from us, no future except in our future—the orphan of the world, he finds with us his home. And with all this, suppose he refuses to be fused into that grand conglomerate we call the "American type." With us, he is not of us. He is original, he has humor, he is tender, he is passive and fiery, he has been

taught what we call justice, and he has his own opinion about it. He has suffered everything a poet, a dramatist, a novelist need suffer before he comes to have his lips anointed. And with it all he is in one sense a spectator, a little out of the race. How would these conditions go towards forming an original development? In a word, suppose the coming novelist is of African origin? When one comes to consider the subject, there is no improbability in it. One thing is certain,—our great novel will not be written by the typical American.

An atypical American, indeed. Not only would the great American novel be written by an African-American, it would be written by an African-American *woman:*

> Yet farther: I have used the generic masculine pronoun because it is convenient; but Fate keeps revenge in store. It was a woman who, taking the wrongs of the African as her theme, wrote the novel that awakened the world to their reality, and why should not the coming novelist be a woman as well as an African? She—the woman of that race—has some claims on Fate which are not yet paid up.

It is these claims on fate that we seek to pay by publishing The Schomburg Library of Nineteenth-Century Black Women Writers.

This theme would be repeated by several black women authors, most notably by Anna Julia Cooper, a prototypical black feminist whose 1892 *A Voice From the South* can be considered to be one of the original texts of the black feminist movement. It was Cooper who first analyzed the fallacy of referring to "the Black man" when speaking of black people and who argued that just as white men cannot speak through the consciousness of black men, neither can black *men* "fully and adequately . . . reproduce the exact Voice of the Black Woman." Gender and race, she argues, cannot be conflated, except in the instance of a black woman's voice, and it is this voice which must be uttered and to which we must listen. As Cooper puts the matter so compellingly:

> It is not the intelligent woman vs. the ignorant woman; nor the white woman vs. the black, the brown, and the red,—it is not even the cause of woman vs. man. Nay, 'tis woman's strongest vindication for speaking that *the world needs to hear her voice*. It would be subversive of every human interest that the cry of one-half the human family be stifled. Woman in stepping from the pedestal of statue-like inactivity in the domestic shrine, and daring to think and move and speak,— to undertake to help shape, mold, and direct the thought of her age, is merely completing the circle of the world's vision. Hers is every interest that has lacked an interpreter and a defender. Her cause is linked with that of every agony that has been dumb—every wrong that needs a voice.
>
> It is no fault of man's that he has not been able to see truth from her standpoint. It does credit both to his head and heart that no greater mistakes have been committed or even wrongs perpetrated while she sat making tatting and snipping paper flowers. Man's own innate chivalry and the mutual interdependence of their interests have insured his treating her cause, in the main at least, as his own. And he is pardonably surprised and even a little chagrined, perhaps, to find his legislation not considered "perfectly lovely" in every respect. But in any case his work is only impoverished by her remaining dumb. The world has had to limp along with the wobbling gait and one-sided hesitancy of a man with one eye. Suddenly the bandage is removed from the other eye and the whole body is filled with light. It sees a circle where before it saw a segment. The darkened eye restored, every member rejoices with it.

The myopic sight of the darkened eye can only be restored when the full range of the black woman's voice, with its own special timbres and shadings, remains mute no longer.

Similarly, Victoria Earle Matthews, an author of short stories and essays, and a cofounder in 1896 of the National Association of Colored Women, wrote in her stunning essay, "The Value of Race Literature" (1895), that "when the literature of our race is developed, it will of necessity be different in all essential points of greatness, true heroism and real Christianity from what we may at the present time, for convenience, call American literature." Matthews argued that this great tradition of Afro-American literature would be the textual outlet "for the unnaturally suppressed inner lives which our people have been compelled to lead." Once these "unnaturally suppressed inner lives" of black people are unveiled, no "grander diffusion of mental light" will shine more brightly, she concludes, than that of the articulate Afro-American woman:

> And now comes the question, What part shall we women play in the Race Literature of the future? . . . within the compass of one small journal ["Woman's Era"] we have struck out a new line of departure—a journal, a record of Race interests gathered from all parts of the United States, carefully selected, moistened, winnowed and garnered by the ablest intellects of educated colored women, shrinking at no lofty theme, shirking no serious duty, aiming at every possible excellence, and determined to do their part in the future uplifting of the race.
>
> If twenty women, by their concentrated efforts in one literary movement, can meet with such success as has engendered, planned out, and so successfully consummated this convention, what much more glorious results, what wider spread success, what grander diffusion of mental light will not come forth at the bidding of the enlarged hosts of women writers, already called into being by the stimulus of your efforts?
>
> And here let me speak one word for my journalistic sisters

who have already entered the broad arena of journalism. Before the "Woman's Era" had come into existence, no one except themselves can appreciate the bitter experience and sore disappointments under which they have at all times been compelled to pursue their chosen vocations.

If their brothers of the press have had their difficulties to contend with, I am here as a sister journalist to state, from the fullness of knowledge, that their task has been an easy one compared with that of the colored woman in journalism.

Woman's part in Race Literature, as in Race building, is the most important part and has been so in all ages. . . . All through the most remote epochs she has done her share in literature. . . .

One of the most important aspects of this set is the republication of the salient texts from 1890 to 1910, which literary historians could well call "The Black Woman's Era." In addition to Mary Helen Washington's definitive edition of Cooper's *A Voice From the South,* we have reprinted two novels by Amelia Johnson, Frances Harper's *Iola Leroy,* two novels by Emma Dunham Kelley, Alice Dunbar-Nelson's two impressive collections of short stories, and Pauline Hopkins's three serialized novels as well as her monumental novel, *Contending Forces*—all published between 1890 and 1910. Indeed, black women published more works of fiction in these two decades than black men had published in the previous half century. Nevertheless, this great achievement has been ignored.

Moreover, the writings of nineteenth-century Afro-American women in general have remained buried in obscurity, accessible only in research libraries or in overpriced and poorly edited reprints. Many of these books have never been reprinted at all; in some instances only one or two copies are extant. In these works of fiction, poetry, autobiography, biography, essays, and journalism resides the mind of the nineteenth-century Afro-American woman. Until these works are made readily available to teachers and their students, a significant segment of the black tradition will remain silent.

Oxford University Press, in collaboration with the Schomburg Center for Research in Black Culture, is publishing thirty volumes of these compelling works, each of which contains an introduction by an expert in the field. The set includes such rare texts as Johnson's *The Hazeley Family* and *Clarence and Corinne*, Plato's *Essays*, the most complete edition of Phillis Wheatley's poems and letters, Emma Dunham Kelley's pioneering novel *Megda*, several previously unpublished stories and a novel by Alice Dunbar-Nelson, and the first collected volumes of Pauline Hopkins's three serialized novels and Frances Harper's poetry. We also present four volumes of poetry by such women as Mary Eliza Tucker Lambert, Adah Menken, Josephine Heard, and Maggie Johnson. Numerous slave and spiritual narratives, a newly discovered novel—*Four Girls at Cottage City*—by Emma Dunham Kelley (-Hawkins), and the first American edition of *Wonderful Adventures of Mrs. Seacole in Many Lands* are also among the texts included.

In addition to resurrecting the works of black women authors, it is our hope that this set will facilitate the resurrection of the Afro-American woman's literary tradition itself by unearthing its nineteenth-century roots. In the works of Nella Larsen and Jessie Fauset, Zora Neale Hurston and Ann Petry, Lorraine Hansberry and Gwendolyn Brooks, Paule Marshall and Toni Cade Bambara, Audre Lorde and Rita Dove, Toni Morrison and Alice Walker, Gloria Naylor and Jamaica Kincaid, these roots have branched luxuriantly. The eighteenth- and nineteenth-century authors whose works are presented in this set founded and nurtured the black women's literary tradition, which must be revived, explicated, analyzed, and debated before we can understand more completely the formal shaping of this tradition within a tradition, a coded literary universe through which, regrettably, we are only just beginning to navigate our way. As Anna Cooper said nearly one hundred years ago, we have been blinded by the loss of sight in one eye and have therefore been unable to detect the full *shape* of the Afro-American literary tradition.

Literary works configure into a tradition not because of some mystical collective unconscious determined by the biology of race or gender, but because writers read other writers and *ground* their representations of experience in models of language provided largely by other writers to whom they feel akin. It is through this mode of literary revision, amply evident in the *texts* themselves—in formal echoes, recast metaphors, even in parody—that a "tradition" emerges and defines itself.

This is formal bonding, and it is only through formal bonding that we can know a literary tradition. The collective publication of these works by black women now, for the first time, makes it possible for scholars and critics, male and female, black and white, to *demonstrate* that black women writers read, and revised, other black women writers. To demonstrate this set of formal literary relations is to demonstrate that sexuality, race, and gender are both the condition and the basis of *tradition*—but tradition as found in discrete acts of language use.

A word is in order about the history of this set. For the past decade, I have taught a course, first at Yale and then at Cornell, entitled "Black Women and Their Fictions," a course that I inherited from Toni Morrison, who developed it in the mid-1970s for Yale's Program in Afro-American Studies. Although the course was inspired by the remarkable accomplishments of black women novelists since 1970, I gradually extended its beginning date to the late nineteenth century, studying Frances Harper's *Iola Leroy* and Anna Julia Cooper's *A Voice From the South,* both published in 1892. With the discovery of Harriet E. Wilson's seminal novel, *Our Nig* (1859), and Jean Yellin's authentication of Harriet Jacobs's brilliant slave narrative, *Incidents in the Life of a Slave Girl* (1861), a survey course spanning over a century and a quarter emerged.

But the discovery of *Our Nig,* as well as the interest in nineteenth-century black women's writing that this discovery generated, convinced me that even the most curious and diligent scholars knew very little of the extensive history of the creative writings of Afro-American women before 1900. Indeed, most scholars of Afro-American literature had never even read most of the books published by black women, simply because these books—of poetry, novels, short stories, essays, and autobiography—were mostly accessible only in rare book sections of university libraries. For reasons unclear to me even today, few of these marvelous renderings of the Afro-American woman's consciousness were reprinted in the late 1960s and early 1970s, when so many other texts of the Afro-American literary tradition were resurrected from the dark and silent graveyard of the out-of-print and were reissued in facsimile editions aimed at the hungry readership for canonical texts in the nascent field of black studies.

So, with the help of several superb research assistants—including David Curtis, Nicola Shilliam, Wendy Jones, Sam Otter, Janadas Devan, Suvir Kaul, Cynthia Bond, Elizabeth Alexander, and Adele Alexander—and with the expert advice of scholars such as William Robinson, William Andrews, Mary Helen Washington, Maryemma Graham, Jean Yellin, Houston A. Baker, Jr., Richard Yarborough, Hazel Carby, Joan R. Sherman, Frances Foster, and William French, dozens of bibliographies were used to compile a list of books written or narrated by black women mostly before 1910. Without the assistance provided through this shared experience of scholarship, the scholar's true legacy, this project could not have been conceived. As the list grew, I was struck by how very many of these titles that I, for example, had never even heard of, let alone read, such as Ann Plato's *Essays*, Louisa Picquet's slave narrative, or Amelia Johnson's two novels, *Clarence and Corinne* and *The Hazeley Family*. Through our research with the Black Periodical Fiction and Poetry Project (funded by NEH and the Ford Foundation), I also realized that several novels by black women, including three works of fiction by Pauline Hopkins, had been serialized in black periodicals, but had never been collected and published as books. Nor had the several books of poetry published by black women, such as the prolific Frances E. W. Harper, been collected and edited. When I discovered still another "lost" novel by an Afro-American woman (*Four Girls at Cottage City*, published in 1898 by Emma Dunham Kelley-Hawkins), I decided to attempt to edit a collection of reprints of these works and to publish them as a "library" of black women's writings, in part so that I could read them myself.

Convincing university and trade publishers to undertake this project proved to be a difficult task. Despite the commercial success of *Our Nig* and of the several reprint series of women's works (such as Virago, the Beacon Black Women Writers Series, and Rutgers' American Women Writers Series), several presses rejected the project as "too large," "too limited," or as "commercially unviable." Only two publishers recognized the viability and the import of the project and, of these, Oxford's commitment to publish the titles simultaneously as a set made the press's offer irresistible.

While attempting to locate original copies of these exceedingly rare books, I discovered that most of the texts were housed at the Schomburg Center for Research in Black Culture, a branch of The New York Public Library, under the direction of Howard Dodson. Dodson's infectious enthusiasm for the project and his generous collaboration, as well as that of his stellar staff (especially Diana Lachatanere, Sharon Howard, Ellis Haizip, Richard Newman, and Betty Gubert), led to a joint publishing initiative that produced this set as part of the Schomburg's major fund-raising campaign. Without Dodson's foresight and generosity of spirit, the set would not have materialized. Without William P. Sisler's masterful editorship at Oxford and his staff's careful attention to detail, the set would have remained just another grand idea that tends to languish in a scholar's file cabinet.

I would also like to thank Dr. Michael Winston and Dr. Thomas C. Battle, Vice-President of Academic Affairs and the Director of the Moorland-Spingarn Research Center (respectively) at Howard University, for their unending encouragement, support, and collaboration in this project, and Esme E. Bhan at Howard for her meticulous research and bibliographical skills. In addition, I would like to acknowledge the aid of the staff at the libraries of Duke University, Cornell University (especially Tom Weissinger and Donald Eddy), the Boston Public Library, the Western Reserve Historical Society, the Library of Congress, and Yale University. Linda Robbins, Marion Osmun, Sarah Flanagan, and Gerard Case, all members of the staff at Oxford, were extraordinarily effective at coordinating, editing, and producing the various segments of each text in the set. Candy Ruck, Nina de Tar, and Phillis Molock expertly typed reams of correspondence and manuscripts connected to the project.

I would also like to express my gratitude to my colleagues who edited and introduced the individual titles in the set. Without their attention to detail, their willingness to meet strict deadlines, and their sheer enthusiasm for this project, the set could not have been published. But finally and ultimately, I would hope that the publication of the set would help to generate even more scholarly interest in the black women authors whose work is presented here. Struggling against the seemingly insurmountable barriers of racism *and* sexism, while often raising families and fulfilling full-time professional obligations, these women managed nevertheless to record their thoughts and feelings and to *testify* to all who dare read them that the will to harness the power of collective endurance and survival is the will to write.

The Schomburg Library of Nineteenth-Century Black Women Writers is dedicated in memory of Pauline Augusta Coleman Gates, who died in the spring of 1987. It was she who inspired in me the love of learning and the love of literature. I have encountered in the books of this set no will more determined, no courage more noble, no mind more sublime, no self more celebratory of the achievements of all Afro-American women, and indeed of life itself, than her own.

A NOTE FROM
THE SCHOMBURG CENTER

Howard Dodson

The Schomburg Center for Research in Black Culture, The New York Public Library, is pleased to join with Dr. Henry Louis Gates and Oxford University Press in presenting The Schomburg Library of Nineteenth-Century Black Women Writers. This thirty-volume set includes the work of a generation of black women whose writing has only been available previously in rare book collections. The materials reprinted in twenty-four of the thirty volumes are drawn from the unique holdings of the Schomburg Center.

A research unit of The New York Public Library, the Schomburg Center has been in the forefront of those institutions dedicated to collecting, preserving, and providing access to the records of the black past. In the course of its two generations of acquisition and conservation activity, the Center has amassed collections totaling more than 5 million items. They include over 100,000 bound volumes, 85,000 reels and sets of microforms, 300 manuscript collections containing some 3.5 million items, 300,000 photographs and extensive holdings of prints, sound recordings, film and videotape, newspapers, artworks, artifacts, and other book and nonbook materials. Together they vividly document the history and cultural heritages of people of African descent worldwide.

Though established some sixty-two years ago, the Center's book collections date from the sixteenth century. Its oldest item, an Ethiopian Coptic Tunic, dates from the eighth or ninth century. Rare materials, however, are most available for the nineteenth-century African-American experience. It is from these holdings that the majority of the titles selected for inclusion in this set are drawn.

The nineteenth century was a formative period in African-American literary and cultural history. Prior to the Civil War, the majority of black Americans living in the United States were held in bondage. Law and practice forbade teaching them to read or write. Even after the war, many of the impediments to learning and literary productivity remained. Nevertheless, black men and women of the nineteenth century persevered in both areas. Moreover, more African-Americans than we yet realize turned their observations, feelings, social viewpoints, and creative impulses into published works. In time, this nineteenth-century printed record included poetry, short stories, histories, novels, autobiographies, social criticism, and theology, as well as economic and philosophical treatises. Unfortunately, much of this body of literature remained, until very recently, relatively inaccessible to twentieth-century scholars, teachers, creative artists, and others interested in black life. Prior to the late 1960s, most Americans (black as well as white) had never heard of these nineteenth-century authors, much less read their works.

The civil rights and black power movements created unprecedented interest in the thought, behavior, and achievements of black people. Publishers responded by revising traditional texts, introducing the American public to a new generation of African-American writers, publishing a variety of thematic anthologies, and reprinting a plethora of "classic texts" in African-American history, literature, and art. The reprints usually appeared as individual titles or in a series of bound volumes or microform formats.

The Schomburg Center, which has a long history of supporting publishing that deals with the history and culture of Africans in diaspora, became an active participant in many of the reprint revivals of the 1960s. Since hard copies of original printed works are the preferred formats for producing facsimile reproductions, publishers frequently turned to the Schomburg Center for copies of these original titles. In addition to providing such material, Schomburg Center staff members offered advice and consultation, wrote introductions, and occasionally entered into formal copublishing arrangements in some projects.

Most of the nineteenth-century titles reprinted during the 1960s, however, were by and about black men. A few black women were included in the longer series, but works by lesser known black women were generally overlooked. The Schomburg Library of Nineteenth-Century Black Women Writers is both a corrective to these previous omissions and an important contribution to Afro-American literary history in its own right. Through this collection of volumes, the thoughts, perspectives, and creative abilities of nineteenth-century African-American women, as captured in books and pamphlets published in large part before 1910, are again being made available to the general public. The Schomburg Center is pleased to be a part of this historic endeavor.

I would like to thank Professor Gates for initiating this project. Thanks are due both to him and Mr. William P. Sisler of Oxford University Press for giving the Schomburg Center an opportunity to play such a prominent role in the set. Thanks are also due to my colleagues at The New York Public Library and the Schomburg Center, especially Dr. Vartan Gregorian, Richard De Gennaro, Paul Fasana, Betsy

Pinover, Richard Newman, Diana Lachatanere, Glenderlyn Johnson, and Harold Anderson for their assistance and support. I can think of no better way of demonstrating than in this set the role the Schomburg Center plays in assuring that the black heritage will be available for future generations.

INTRODUCTION

Kenny J. Williams

In 1841 Ann Plato's *Essays; Including Biographies and Miscellaneous Pieces, in Prose and Poetry* appeared. Printed for the author at Hartford, Connecticut, and containing an introduction by the famous abolitionist, Reverend Dr. James W. C. Pennington, the work not only reveals much about an extraordinary black woman but also reminds us once again of the city—now overshadowed by other urban centers—that was a cultural center of the new nation. In many ways, Hartford, its Congregationalism, its free black society relatively secure within itself, and a local literary tradition—all seemingly disconnected forces—produced Ann Plato. These disparate elements may not have caused her to become a writer, but they certainly provide insight into the background from which she came. At the same time, certain theories concerning assimilation and prevailing attitudes about Afro-American writers undoubtedly have obscured for future generations both her life and her work.

I

Less heterogenous than Boston and larger than Salem in neighboring Massachusetts, initially not as tolerant of "outsiders" as New Haven, with which it served as the joint capital of Connecticut throughout the eighteenth century to several years after the Civil War, Hartford in the 1840s was a major New England city. Although a small group of colonists settled in the region in 1635, Thomas Hooker is considered the founder of the Hartford colony. Leading his parishioners out of the Massachusetts Bay area in 1636, the learned minister's views on religion were not compatible with what he deemed the inconsistencies of the Boston Puritans. The settlers of Hartford, in conjunction with others nearby, realized that they were not subject to the laws of Massachusetts and drew up Connecticut's Fundamental Orders, a document that called into question the theocratic beliefs of New England by supporting a principle that Americans now have come to take for granted: "The foundation of authority [in government] is in the free consent of the people."

Despite evidences of religious intolerance (not unusual in colonial America), Hartford was marked throughout its formative period—as were many other New England towns—by unresolved paradoxes. Nominally committed to freedom, it willingly restricted freedom to a select group. Although the place was a center for individual rights, women and children had few privileges. Men were in complete control; even their entitlement to their wives' property was protected by law. And unless members of relatively affluent households, children had little time for the imagined pleasures of youth. In this agricultural community, they were put to work early in their lives. Later, with the advent of industrialism, child labor went unchecked, hence, few children were able to attend school with any degree of regularity. In time, while the young men of means might go off to Yale College in New Haven or attend another such institution, the young women would simply be drilled, usually at home, in the basics. Some were fortunate enough to attend school for such training. But whether they were educated at home or in a seminary, showing proficiency in the domestic arts, such as needlework, was the mark of a lady. Consequently, for a number of years, an "educated" woman was a rarity.

Just as Connecticut was slow to grant rights to women and children so also was its small black population limited by the laws and customs of the state. But given the proscriptions of many communities, there was a degree of enlightenment in the Hartford area. Although the state did little to include blacks within its body politic, Connecticut was concerned enough about human rights to have incorporated within its statutes several laws providing for the rights of slaves and limiting the degree to which they could be mistreated. Furthermore, there was a program of automatic manumission that applied to slave children born after March 1, 1784, mandating that they would become free when they reached twenty-five years of age. Admittedly, nineteenth-century statistical records are frequently incomplete; however, although slavery itself was legal until 1848, the 1820 census reveals that among the less than 8,000 blacks in the state, only ninety-seven were slaves. By 1848 there were twenty such restricted human beings. Free blacks, then, formed the larger segment of Connecticut's early nineteenth-century black population. That they were concentrated in cities like Hartford should come as no surprise. Thus, by the 1840s and despite whatever notions the region might have had about its democratic nature, the fact is that there was, as one might expect, several components of its two-class society not all of which were mutually exclusive: men and women, the well-to-do and the poor, blacks and whites.

Although it might be said that Connecticut treated blacks with benign neglect—for, by exclusion, few of the state's provisions applied to its black population—the state did not drastically hamper development. In fact, it interestingly supported an event whose description ranges from the pejorative to the laudatory. It is generally well known that in the early towns and villages of New England, one of the important annual activities revolved around "Election Day" for both political and military units. The special sermons were often accompanied by parades for the occasions, and other such festivities were common. Less well known is the fact that among blacks in Connecticut there was a parallel activity that was sanctioned by white society. The Hartford *Daily Courant* ran an article on "Black Governors in Connecticut" by Scaeva (the pseudonym for Isaac W. Stuart), which was subsequently included in the 1853 publication, *Hartford in the Olden Time* edited by W. M. B. Hartley (pp. 37–44). Mary K. Talcott revealed in her "Hartford in the Revolution" (which appears in *Hartford in History: A Series of Papers* by Resident Authors [Hartford: n.p., 1899]) that "this custom of electing a governor, in imitation of the whites, had been observed by the [N]egroes for a number of years, and the fortunate individual was always treated with great attention and support by his colored brethren" (pp. 209–10). The event was the occasion for gala celebrations, and the person so elected had great authority.

Just when the practice of electing black governors began is not clear. Many historic descriptions are derisive, with some later nineteenth-century historians referring to the custom as the "Nigger Election." They saw only the festivities and imitation without realizing that these events could be viewed as a type of safety valve. Nonetheless, for a number of years these exercises in self-government were held in Hartford. Reprehensible though it may appear to modern readers, the activity provided an important ritual in one process of self-determination—even if by imitation. Although it is impossible to determine with certainty the effects of such affairs on the black population, it might be safe to conclude that they made the distinction between those who governed and those who were the governed more immediate while providing a nominal sense of participation.

spite Hartford's attempt to finance a separate school system, educational opportunities were limited for blacks. In fact, there were general bans that limited blacks' access to the common provisions of the state. In the absence of some regulatory statutes designed to be all inclusive, black family units and black churches developed sophisticated plans for self-help. These private enterprises led to the development of an articulate black elite in spite of white laws and white attitudes.

The church—like the family—was an important institution and was the center of social as well as intellectual life in Hartford. Not unexpectedly, the clergy played conspicuous roles in the community. Congregationalism, which until the Connecticut Constitution of 1818 was the state church, was the heir of the old Puritan tradition that had produced Thomas Hooker and his followers. Although it rejected a rigid ecclesiastical hierarchy, the Congregational Church of Connecticut was frequently as doctrinaire as other religious groups. Some churches maintained "African corners" for their black parishioners, others admitted blacks to unrestricted membership; and even within Congregationalism itself there developed a black church with a highly educated clergy. One such church was Hartford's Colored Congregational Church, pastored for a period by the Reverend Dr. James W. C. Pennington.

By the nineteenth century, the community's ambivalence in matters of race was apparent. Whatever personal beliefs were held by its members, the Congregational church itself was strongly identified with the antislavery movement. While some men in Hartford spent much time arguing abstractly about the role of God in human affairs, such men as Horace Bushnell (1802–1876)—in his concern about urban life— were quite cognizant of the fact that the welfare of Hartford's black population had to be considered. Nonetheless, others held strong convictions concerning what was presumed to be the innate inferiority of blacks that supported the need for separation at the same time there was a continuing support for human rights. Despite obvious contradictions between the theory of race and some day-to-day practices, Hartford became a place of great antislavery sentiments and much visible activity. Many of the leadership roles were filled by the black clergy. At the same time, such men and women as Frederick Douglass and Maria Stewart, who lectured there frequently, were often entertained in the city. In the process of its development, Hartford never had eruptions of the more violent types of racial animosities that marked New York, Philadelphia, and other nineteenth-century Northern cities.

In addition to its "progress" in racial matters, for a number of years Hartford was a literary center not only of the colonial period but also of the new nation. From the beginning of its history, Hartford supported a number of writers and printing houses. Thomas Hooker, who delivered learned sermons that rivaled those produced by the Mather dynasty, was probably the city's first important writer. His published sermons were widely circulated. He is best known in American literature for his *A Survey of the Summe of Church Discipline* (1648) in which he set forth the nature of Congregationalism and defined it in terms of human nature as well as human reason. Throughout the seventeenth century, religious treatises with political overtones were popular. Hooker was followed by a group of eighteenth- and nineteenth-century clergymen, including James W. C. Pennington, who made Hartford a nucleus for a particular type of religious discourse.

It was in Hartford that a group of the city's late eighteenth-century residents addressed the issue of a national literature. They fully understood political independence would mean little without cultural independence. Such men as John Trumbull (1750–1831), Colonel David Humphreys (1753–1831), Joel Barlow (1755–1812), Dr. Lemuel Hopkins (1750–1801), and Timothy Dwight (1752–1817) were active in business, political, and religious circles. Known to later generations as the Hartford or Connecticut Wits, individually they produced several significant works in colonial American literature, although collectively they issued some of the most forgettable poetry celebrating the new United States. Yet, the shortcomings of *The Anarchiad* (1786), *The Political Greenhouse* (1799), and *The Echo* (1807) do not conceal their commitment to the creation of a national literature through the use of national events and concerns. Often demonstrating elements of wit, they relied heavily upon the importance of setting or locale rather than language.

During this period, two other residents of the city were making contributions that were ultimately to influence the nation's literary history. Noah Webster (1758–1843), perhaps best known for his spelling books and dictionary of English as the language was used in the New World, declared in his *Dissertations On the English Language* (1789) that an American literature could not develop until there was an acceptance of American English as a viable vehicle for creative work. And although one might wonder how much the many volumes of "Peter Parley" affected young women like Ann Plato—and even the exact number of books by Samuel Griswold Goodrich (1793–1860) now seems to be in dispute—it is likely that he wrote under that pseudonym almost 200 books dedicated to upright living and to such virtues as were usually set forth for the young. While Webster was concerned with a stabilization of language, a subject perhaps of more interest to the linguistics specialist, Goodrich created a popular tradition for a certain type of moralistic literature.

By the nineteenth century, the city also supported a group of women writers, many of whom were also extremely active in movements in support of women's rights. Although the poetry of Lydia Huntley Sigourney (1791–1865), often called "The Sweet Singer of Hartford," and Emma Willard (1787–1870), best known for her still popular "Rocked in the Cradle of the Deep," is seldom read today, the two women did much to prove the literary capabilities of women as writers. Their work was complemented later by that of Catherine Beecher (1800–1878) who specifically advocated educational reforms and addressed issues of both race and gender. During the formative period of the so-called Local Color Movement, Harriet Beecher Stowe (1812–1896) and Rose Terry Cooke (1827–1892) made long-lasting contributions to the literary image of New England.

If the work of the Hartford Wits, Noah Webster, Peter Parley, and some vocal women can be considered a distinctive step in the history of American literature, the city was also important for a parallel development in the evolution of Afro-American literature. It was in Hartford that Jupiter Hammon, an early slave poet, published four broadsides: "An Address to Miss Phillis Wheatly [*sic*]" (1778), "An Essay on the Ten Virgins" (1779), "A Winter Piece" (1782), and "An Evening's Improvement," which contains the poetic dialogue "The Kind Master and Dutiful Servant" (n.d.).

Some modern Afro-Americanists would prefer to overlook the life and works of Jupiter Hammon, mistakenly called by some "America's First Negro Poet"; but the fact remains that when his owners moved from Long Island to Connecticut in order to escape the immediacy of the Revolutionary War, it was in Hartford that he wrote his major existing works and had them printed as broadsides. According to Hammon, his work was well received, and its very existence attests undoubtedly to some early interest in it. This becomes significant because, when coupled with the reception that Phillis Wheatley's far more sophisticated work received, it might suggest an audience for black writers.

Consequently, by the 1840s not only was the population of Hartford augmented by a small, but active, black community, but also there had been established separate viable literary traditions: one white, the other black. Perhaps as symbolic of this separation as anything else is Rev. Charles W. Everest's *Poets of Connecticut*. Published at Hartford in 1843 by the company of Case, Tiffany, and Burnham, it contains the work of forty-three poets, six of whom are women. It does not include any of the work of Ann Plato nor that of any black. While admittedly an anthologist or an editor has the right of selectivity, in many ways Rev. Everest's book is thus representative of the doctrine of omission that causes one of the central problems in the reconstruction of the history of Afro-American literature.

II

As the productions of early Afro-American writers have become more available, there has been a slow recognition—

bestowed begrudgingly at times, to be sure—that these works extend beyond the eighteenth-century poetry of Phillis Wheatley or the verse, fiction, and essays of Paul Laurence Dunbar written more than one hundred years later. If there occurred any natural curiosity about the obvious gap in Afro-American literary history between the death of Wheatley in 1784 and the publication of Dunbar's *Oak and Ivy* in 1892, until very recently few voiced it. A study of the literary histories of the nineteenth century and the growing number in the twentieth reveals the silence of scholarship. Even the carefully crafted *Literary History of the United States* in the mid-years of the twentieth century, known not only for its analyses of the so-called major figures but also for its inclusion of writing that the more charitable critics call "nonliterary," pays little attention to the Afro-American writer.

While the silence of scholarship has been a problem, the study of Afro-American writing has also been hampered by two equally damaging approaches. There are those who automatically assume that if a piece comes from a black it is good only insofar as it expresses some explanation of the black condition in America. Liberally applying sociological criticism, such critics search each work for evidence of often strongly held, preconceived notions. Then there are those who decree with the authority of American racism that little of literary merit or worth can come from a black writer. For this latter group it has been a popular technique to make comparisons between black writers and their counterparts not only in the United States but also in England. As a result, declarations have been made about the lack of literary standards, and apologies have been offered in order to make the expected dismissals. Later comparisons were made using Hawthorne or Melville or some other assumed major writer— but always with the same result.

It was not until the Harlem Renaissance that there were some changes. After the intense interest in Afro-American literature developed, several works dealing with black writers appeared. Four major anthologies were published during the 1920s; however, James Weldon Johnson's *The Book of American Negro Poetry* (1922), Robert Kerlin's *Negro Poets and Their Poems* (1923), *An Anthology of Verse by American Negroes* (1924) edited by Newman Ivey White and Walter Clinton Jackson, as well as Countee Cullen's *Caroling Dusk* (1927) primarily showcased the poetry written by men. Furthermore, with few exceptions, the interest that existed in Afro-American poetry tended to begin with studies of Dunbar. When Benjamin Brawley, professor of English at Howard University, issued his *Early Negro American Writers* in 1935, there was an attempt to alter this trend. As part of his prefatory remarks, he acknowledged: "We at once face the fact that, judged by artistic standards, much of this early writing is weak. Some of it, however, is good, and what is lacking in literary quality is in general more than made up in social interest." Brawley said that he "hoped" that his work would "be of service to the student of the history of the Negro as well as to one concerned with literary values only." His early research led him to understand something of the extent of early Afro-American writing, and he concluded that during the antebellum period "much that should be included is reflective of the agitation that preceded the Civil War" (p. v).

Given his era and the limited work done on Afro-American writers up to his time, Brawley was correct in asserting: "I have once more been reminded how much of the writing about representative Negroes has been superficial and inaccurate." Whether or not he knew the work of earlier critics probably is unimportant in the great scheme of things. But many of them really can be accused of presenting, as Brawley said, "superficial and inaccurate" information. For example, Kerlin in his *Negro Poets and their Poems* incorrectly identified Ann Plato as "a slave girl who published a book of twenty poems in 1841" (p. 24); however, Loggins, whose *The Negro Author in America* (1931) is often patronizing, did at least mention Ann Plato and recognized her work as the "only . . . book written by an American Negro between 1840 and 1865 which was avowedly issued as a collection of essays" (p. 248). Only White and Jackson, in the brief biographical and critical summaries of selected writers that appear in their *An Anthology of Verse by American Negroes,* seemed to have understood the extent of Ann Plato's work even though they did not include her poems in their anthology; yet they mistakenly dismissed her poems as "earnest, illiterate, and vapid, with occasional errors in grammar and spelling, and strained rhymes" and referred to her essays as "commonplace" (p. 230). Johnson's anthology tends to be broader in scope than Countee Cullen's and acknowledges—at least in a limited way—the versifiers of earlier periods; yet both focus heavily upon their own contemporaries of the Harlem Renaissance and obviously do not cite Ann Plato. Although Brawley's definition of "representative Negroes" was not set forth, his "early Negro writers" included twenty-one writers—nineteen men and two women. Ann Plato was not among the latter. Clearly, all of these works ultimately raise a significant question, the answer to which would condition subsequent accounts. Is it better for a writer to be identified incorrectly, or ignored completely? When Ann Plato has been mentioned, it has usually been without a firm understanding of either her work or what she represented; on the other hand, generally her work has been disregarded—either by accident or by design.

That the study of nineteenth-century Afro-American literature has been dominated by male slave writers such as Jupiter
Hammon and George Moses Horton and ex-slaves such as
Frederick Douglass and William Wells Brown is a fact. No
matter how one might assess the "literary" contributions of
them or of Benjamin Banneker, Richard Allen, Absalom
Jones, Prince Hall, David Walker, and Martin R. Delany,
these men often form a core around which many of the
discussions of early black writers revolve. Certainly, in many
indisputable ways, the poetry of James M. Whitfield, Daniel
Payne, James Madison Bell, George B. Vashon, and Charles
Reason demonstrates a certain sophistication that is frequently
overlooked in our latter-day search for alleged "spokesmen
of the black experience," but also their work gives clues as
to the scope and diversity of Afro-American writing. On the
other hand, discussions of black women are generally reduced
to considerations of Phillis Wheatley and Frances Ellen Watkins Harper with perhaps a passing reference to Lucy Terry's
historic—if not aesthetic—"Bars Fight." Black women writers have not only suffered the indignities fostered by matters
of race but also have been subjected to the male chauvinism
of both white and black critics.

Although few of the nineteenth-century Afro-American
writers will become household names in the foreseeable future, many left enough records of themselves that a reconstruction, partial though it may be, of their lives and times
is possible. Thus, there is a sense of knowing them. However,
Ann Plato, about whom little is actually known, presents a
different case, and consideration of her work raises more
questions than there are available answers. Legitimately readers may ask: Who was she? When was she born? When did
she die? Did she live in Hartford, Connecticut, all of her

life? Did she decide to write because Hartford was a cultural center of some dimension? Was she inspired by the literary ferment that had been a traditional part of the city? Or was she motivated purely by a religious calling? Did she expect to sell her *Essays?* If so, who was her probable audience?

She obviously was part of the small black community of Hartford, a community that had had a relatively long history of freedom in the region. As a member of the Congregational Church, she was a spiritual descendant of Thomas Hooker and as much given to examinations of piety as was he. What she actually believed about writing as a creative or commemorative act is difficult to determine. There is some indication in her poetry that she had a concern about the nature of posterity, although the nationalism of the Hartford Wits is absent from her work. At the same time, she did not exhibit a strong belief in a distinct Afro-American literature. Maybe there were enough writers around her to suggest that she did not feel it necessary to comment upon the uniqueness of her work. Furthermore, she must have had a certain self-assurance, despite avowals of humility, that made her think her work had some measure of worth. On the other hand, readers often bring preconceptions to a work. Because we have expected written records to display overt evidence not only of time and place but also of race and gender, we have become uncomfortable when they do not. That she was a woman of nineteenth-century New England is fairly certain, but seldom does her work deal with racial matters.

In the absence of contemporaneous documents, attempting to reconstruct a life is as difficult as trying to find the proverbial needle in a haystack. Certainly when that life does not leave an inordinate number of clues or when it seems to send mixed signals, reconstruction seems little more than an exercise in futility. Ann Plato's life essentially must be determined from *Essays; Including Biographies and Miscellaneous Pieces, in Prose and Poetry,* her only known publication, since she apparently left no other records.

If the existing records are accurate, several Plato families lived in the Hartford area for a number of years. Some belonged to the First Congregational Church of Old Lyme, others lived in Hartford. While Ann Plato's identity remains unclear, there are some possible observations that can be made about her from the introduction to her work as well as from the work itself. Following a custom still in vogue, her collection of essays and poems contains a preface by a well-known person of her day. As a communicant of the Colored Congregational Church of Hartford, pastored by the Reverend Dr. James W. C. Pennington, she undoubtedly knew of his influence and national reputation. In the 1840s, he was considered to be one of the powerful and effective clergymen of the era. He apparently lived in Hartford from 1840 until 1845, delivering what was printed as "A Farewell Sermon Preached in the Fifth Congregational Church, November 2, 1845." While pastoring in Hartford, he published some of his significant works. Perhaps as a carryover from the Puritan Plain Style and the rhetoric of "instruction" as a primary goal of writing, Pennington in his brief *Covenants Involving Moral Wrong Are Not Obligatory Upon Man* (1842) tried to reduce the devotional and the spiritual aspects of life to their most simple precepts. Originally delivered as a sermon, it demonstrates the kind of ecclesiastical disputation that we have come to expect—either rightly or wrongly—from New England. Perhaps of even greater importance is his *A Text Book of t. Origins and History . . . of the Colored People,* which appeared a year earlier in 1841. He traveled extensively, giving lectures in the cause of the antislavery movement. In 1849, while he was in England, his narrative, *The Fugitive Blacksmith; or, Events in the Life of James W. C. Pennington,* appeared.

Obviously the preacher, who was famous enough to receive later an honorary degree from the University of Heidelberg, felt he knew Ann Plato well enough to write the introduction to her book, and it is perhaps from him—at least in part—that she has received some validation. Clearly, she was a young woman in his church whose devotion apparently impressed him. His own didactic style seems to have found an apt pupil in Plato, as one might understand from Pennington's effusive preface that seems as much a defense as an introduction. Yet, even Pennington failed to answer many of the questions that remain about her. Of importance to him was the establishment of Ann Plato not only as a communicant of his church but also as "a colored lady." That he felt it necessary to attest to her race permits him to declare that she wishes "to accomplish something for the credit of her people" and counters the notion that "nature has done nothing but fit us for *slaves.*" He assures readers that she is "of pleasing piety and modest worth." For reasons now lost to history, he found her "interesting" even though her religious messages seem more related to Jupiter Hammon's work than to that of the minister whom she evidently admired. He apparently recognized her imperfections and was under no illusion that she had produced a finished work, but he praised her literary attempts and asked that she be encouraged because "[t]he best way to do justice to young writers is to weigh their thoughts without so strict a regard to their style as we should pay in the case of elder writers." Citing "Philis Wheatly [*sic*], . . . Terence, and Capitain, and Francis Williams" as her forerunners, he especially likens her to Wheatley because Ann "is passionately fond of reading." Whatever Plato's shortcomings, in a rare display of wit, albeit forced, Pennington asks: "But as Greece had a Plato why may we not have a Platoess?"

Given the New England tendency to put pen to paper as the elect and nonelect of the seventeenth century tried to examine their lives and the lives of others for evidences of God's grace, given the eighteenth century's continuing interest in documenting the will of God, it is not surprising that this young woman—obviously a product of a certain religious fundamentalism—engaged in such an exercise in the nineteenth century. What, however, might surprise modern readers is her apparent belief that she had something of significance to say that warranted having it printed. Yet, when one considers the availability of printing presses and the fashionable tendency to commit thoughts for posterity, Ann Plato seems to be following a convention that had had greatest vogue in the previous century and continued into the early years of the nineteenth century. The fact that there does not seem to be a second book may mean that she failed to get the necesssary patronage to make such a work possible. She may have disappeared somewhere in Europe. She may have moved to the West or to Canada. Or she may have died. Whatever her fate, at a given moment Hartford had, as indicated by Pennington, "its Platoess," an overstatement that does not seem peculiar to Afro-American literature if one remembers that Anne Bradstreet was called "the tenth muse lately sprung up in America."

As essays go, hers are not spectacular, but they certainly are not "illiterate." Yet, at no point would she be compared to Maria Stewart, who did so much for the essay in America prior to Ralph Waldo Emerson. Instead, hers are pedestrian devotional exercises that are by and large grammatically correct. The sixteen didactic essays are simple in style and uncomplicated in thought. Their merit rests in the fact that they have been preserved and display some historic continuity between the early Afro-American writers and those of the post-Civil War period.

Plato's general philosophy seems to have been based upon a Christianity that relied heavily upon such concepts as obedience, devotion, unquestioned respect for authority. The racial issues that affected Pennington greatly did not seem to influence Plato's work. Obviously born free, she would not have been, in all probability, as aware of the psychological depths of slavery as was Pennington, a former slave, because she would not have known enough slaves to measure the effects of America's "peculiar institution," nor would she have deemed from the "freedom" of Hammon or Wheatley the extent of the degradation associated with forced servitude. Nonetheless, her prose might suggest to some readers that she was also oblivious to many of the activities in Hartford. Thus we do not get a strong sense of the everyday life and concerns of the community. Yet her essays reveal, in addition to the strong religious element, an educational level that would have placed her above most women—black or white—of her era.

III

Matters of religion and patterns for good living tend to dominate *Essays; Including Biographies and Miscellaneous Pieces, in Prose and Poetry*. Although occasionally prone to the use of epigrams, some of her essays seem especially well constructed. "Religion" discusses obedience as a duty of the Christian and emphasizes the importance of worship. She personifies *religion* as "the daughter of Heaven" and presents the same ambiguity to be found in the fundamentalism of Jupiter Hammon, although she is clearly better educated than Hammon. Yet she is convinced that religion prepares one for the happiness of heaven, and life is but an interlude. Much of the same argument is presented in "Obedience," which stresses not only the importance of being obedient to parents but also declares that a lack of obedience is in actuality sinful. "Benevolence" attempts to explicate the Golden Rule and speaks positively of—among others—John Elliott, who for many years served as a gospel minister to the Indians of the region. However limited his success, he has become known for his preservation of an Indian language through his translation of the Scriptures. "Employment of Time" proposes a guide to good living in which one gives the first hour of the day to God. In dealing with the order of life, she declares in "The Seasons" that changes in nature exemplify the shifts in human existence. All of these essays say exactly what one would expect a pious young New England woman of the early nineteenth century to say.

For many reasons "Education" is one of her significant and most representative essays. While it assumed the usual Africa-as-the-dark-continent position that was so prominent in the work of American evangelicals of the nineteenth century and expresses her pride in those zealous Christian missionaries who willingly sacrificed the comforts of home to "carr[y] a message of love to the burning climes of Africa," the essay also suggests the extent of her own knowledge. The allusions contained in the piece indicate at least a cursory understanding of the classics, geography, history, science, and literature.

Like others of her generation, she viewed education as a means of advancement and stressed the importance of books as lasting cultural artifacts. Recognizing the popularity of the oral literary tradition, she argues—quite correctly—that such a tradition can benefit only one era; hence, it is important to preserve books, the "silent teachers," in order to pass knowledge from one generation to another. As on other occasions, she also makes it clear that she is a part of the United States and refers to the first settlers of "our" country. That sense of belonging eliminates a sense of alienation that was to become characteristic of the work of so many black women writers. Not only does she stress the importance of education for young people but also examines its relationship to religion, a concept central to the descendants of seventeenth-century fundamentalism.

"Decision of Character," which emphasizes the importance of determination in permitting one to overcome adversity, uses a series of illustrative figures to support her idea. Once again, the range of allusions (Columbus, Demosthenes, Pompey, Benjamin Franklin, Fulton, Robert Bruce) suggests a survey of her own knowledge and learning. In "Diligence and Negligence" and "Two School Girls" she alters her usual style of exposition. The former is presented in the dialogue mode. The latter is a first-person narrative that tells of an acquaintance while repeating her theme of the importance of knowledge. In a moment of optimism, unwarranted though it may have been, she is convinced that conditions are improving for women.

In addition to the sixteen essays, there are four brief biographies of young women who were obviously friends, but the significance of their lives was not established by Plato; and if such an importance ever existed, it has been lost. The four of them were obviously pious and heroically went through periods of illness before dying at relatively young ages, ranging from seventeen years of age to twenty-six. The four also seemed to range in economic status; however, all were obviously free. In her usual obscure method of dealing with racial matters, Plato alludes in her biography of Miss Eliza Loomis Sherman (wealthy enough to be in a household with servants) to her subject's illness but reminds her readers that if Eliza had "wished for shelter beneath a Georgia clime, that privilege would not have been granted her, on account of the laws."

The twenty poems in the *Essays* are also an obvious result of her youthful fancy and complete devotion. Pietistic, worshipful, essentially devoid of controversy, they often are concerned with death. To some readers they might seem to be simply exercises in versification. Few of them appeal to the literary tastes and interests of this century, but several include the best of her work. And if her work is to continue to live, it will undoubtedly be based upon these poems rather than her essays. "Reflections, Written on Visiting the Grave of a Venerated Friend" is one such poem. That Ann Plato was preoccupied with death should not be surprising given her time and place. The New England Puritan elegy was a popular literary form, executed by both the literary and the nonliterary as a form of familiar condolence. The eighteenth century produced many formal funeral expressions that view death in a classical and detached manner. Unlike her Puritan forebears, however, Plato followed a far more romantic view of death. Hence in the quatrains (rhyming aabb) of "Reflections, Written on Visiting the Grave of a Venerated Friend" she expresses a very personal view of death. A similar pattern is repeated in "I Have No Brother," apparently a poignant personal reference. Yet, in the former poem, she was not above the hyperbole and forced personification that so characterized the earlier elegies of Wheatley and other neoclassicists in such a stanza as:

> Oh! that the gale that sweeps the heath,
> Too roughly o'er your leaves should breathe,
> Then sigh for her—and when you bloom
> Scatter your fragrance o'er her tomb.

But there is a romantic quality that goes beyond the impersonal, clinical view of death so admired in earlier generations.

For reasons that have nothing to do with its content, "Lines, Written Upon Being Examined in School Studies for the Preparation of a Teacher" suggests an interesting observation can be made about literary influences or literary models. First of all, there is a curious insertion of a probable autobiographical element that asserts the age of Plato's poetic persona: "Now fifteen years their destined course have run,/ In fast succession round the central sun." She then proceeds to speak of the importance of "recollection." It may, of course, be assumed that the poem was written when she was fifteen or sixteen years old. What, however, is more significant is the fact that a similar two lines appear in Wheatley's poem, "On Recollection" in which Wheatley says about her poetic persona "Now eighteen years their destined course have run,/ In fast succession round the central sun." While there is little evidence to prove that Ann Plato knew much about Wheatley or her work, the likelihood is, of course, that she was familiar with both. Pennington even suggests similarities between the two women. Furthermore, Wheatley's death was duly reported in the press, and among some she was a prime example of a talent that had been cut off before its time. However, before it is assumed that Plato "copied" from Wheatley or rushed into print in order to be considered as the direct descendant of Wheatley, it must be remembered that her poetry in many ways is more varied than the strictness of Wheatley's adherence to the neoclassical tradition.

"To the First of August" is one of her few "racial" poems and deals with 1838, the *annus mirabilis,* when slavery was abolished in the British West Indies. Like other Afro-American writers (such as James Madison Bell and James M. Whitfield) who celebrated August 1, 1838, as a portent of what was to come in the United States, she praised England and concluded: "Then let us celebrate the day,/ And lay the thought to heart,/ And teach the rising race the way,/ That they may not depart." Her long and rather ambitious dramatic poem, "The Natives of America," addresses the seldom discussed issue of the reasons for the downfall of the American Indian. In some ways and with some obvious changes, the "cruel oppression" suffered by the Indians could be transferred to the subjugated blacks. It is perhaps in "Forget Me Not" that Ann Plato reached the peak and most innovative point in her creative life. Not content to employ the usual four-line stanza, she utilizes a six-line stanza with the first five lines appearing in a more or less regular iambic tetrameter and the final line in iambic dimeter until the last stanza. In the last stanza, the poem shifts to a five-line form with the last line being written in iambic trimeter. Some might argue convincingly that the poem's structure is merely an accident; others might suggest that in her use of the refrain or repeated last line she shows evidence of Poe's "The Raven." But the fact remains that, in addition to her versification (simplistic though the expressed ideas may be), her use of parallel construction not only in the initial stanza but also as a means

to connect the first seven stanzas, produces a cumulative effect
that may even impress a modern reader who is accustomed to
a more complicated poetic structure.

Certain assumptions can be made about her theory of
poetics. Subjects were not to be solely conditioned by race
or gender, although she has far more poems that suggest
the latter. Either by accident or design, her unrhymed lines
hint at a free verse that was to become important in American
poetry just as her rhyme schemes frequently relied upon the
approximation of vowel sounds rather than a repetition of
them. Furthermore, while decidedly subscribing to the notion
of a special language for poetry, a special poetic diction, she
was not as guided by the strictures of rhythmic techniques as
the neoclassicists had been. Plato chose far more romantic
subjects and was given to the expression of her personal
feelings on various subjects.

IV

In the final analysis, a central question certainly cannot be
resisted: No matter how appealing her work might have been
in the early years of the nineteenth century, why would anyone
wish to read Ann Plato today? She apparently began no school
of writing with followers admitting their indebtedness to her.
Her work does not seem to speak to that concept of univer-
sality so admired by literary historians as the test of merit.
Even the quality of "interest" seems to be missing from so
many of her pieces that are dated by their very presentation.
Neither does she reveal much about the unique Afro-American culture located in Hartford. Perhaps if she had been as
devout in her antislavery sentiments as in her desire for a

Christian life, she would have voiced this concern in her work. Not only would she have been adopted by the abolitionists in order to further their aims, but also her essays and poems undoubtedly would have become part of the nineteenth century's antislavery literature. Rather, she is simply an early example of an apparently young woman determined to live in an antagonistic culture without becoming antagonistic, proving to herself and to her world that the concerns of life are neither "black" nor "white" but are simply human concerns. In an era much given to the presumption that there was, and still is, a single black experience, a period whose knowledge of the past is colored by the notion that prior to the Civil War all blacks were not only slaves but also illiterate, Ann Plato reminds us of the urbanity and piety of New England, and her very existence itself might disclose by implication a great deal about Hartford.

Questions relating to an identification of this woman who wrote with so much assurance and devotion will probably continue to pique the curiosity of those who read *Essays; Including Biographies and Miscellaneous Pieces, in Prose and Poetry*. To have her book as a testimony to her probable existence does not substitute for more detailed information about her. Ultimately, the present generation must try to place Ann Plato within the framework of her predecessors and followers. Certainly, her work does not indicate the scope of learning nor the perfection of technique exhibited by Phillis Wheatley. In comparison, her work seems simplistic and hurried; we do not as yet have a canon as large as that of Wheatley. She does not exhibit the racial commitment or diversity of the outstanding Maria Stewart, whose major work appeared in the 1830s. She certainly is not a Frances Ellen Watkins Harper who apparently achieved a degree of

popularity both before and after the Civil War; but she must
not have been as old as Harper nor had she had the same
experiences. There is much evidence to suggest that Ann
Plato, probably a teacher for a period in her life, had led a
rather sheltered existence. This may account for the fact that
the essays and brief biographical studies are not only predict-
able but also exemplify the kind of introspective exercises that
are popular with certain New England writers. Thus, whatever her views on racial and feminist issues, she managed,
for the most part, to mask them in a cloak of piety.

   Nevertheless, in some ways Plato was the forerunner of
some later writers. The latter part of the nineteenth century
and the early years of the twentieth saw the exquisite lyrics
of Henrietta Cordelia Ray and the sonnets of Mrs. Alice
Dunbar-Nelson. And while it is perhaps too didactic and
simplistic for modern readers, the poetry of Eva A. Jessye
and Mrs. J. W. Hammond illustrates a type of homespun
verse that became popular with some audiences. Hence by
the time of the Harlem Renaissance and the work of that
era's poets such as Georgia Douglas Johnson and Angelina
Grimké of Washington, D.C., Anne Spencer of Lynchburg,
Virginia, and Jessie Fauset of Philadelphia, there had unwit-
tingly developed a particular genre of verse from some black
women. Devoid of great bitterness, much given to nature
studies, occasionally devoted to racial issues, it was a poetry
that by its very existence suggested that such abstract qualities
as life, love, truth, beauty, or even death could transcend the
mundane elements of everyday living. Whether for good or
ill, many of these women accepted a nonracial theory of art
and insisted that there should be no sense of blackness distin-
guishing their writing. Simplistically explained, for them a
daffodil is a daffodil whether the artist is black or white.

Whatever their views on posterity, their works are marked by an earnestness that suggsts a desire to be accepted within the mainstream of American writing without denying their race or their gender. And so it was with Ann Plato. As she examined piety and offered tributes to her friends, as she wrote essays that were in essence catechisms for those who wished to live devout lives, and as she wrote verses on various subjects, she plaintively seems to remind later generations: "Forget me not."

ESSAYS;

INCLUDING

Biographies and Miscellaneous Pieces,

IN

PROSE AND POETRY.

BY ANN PLATO.

HARTFORD.

PRINTED FOR THE AUTHOR.

1841.

CONTENTS.

~~~~~~~~

PROSE.

BIOGRAPHIES.

POETRY.

TO THE READER.

~~~~~~~~~~~~~~~~~~~~~~~~~~~~~~~

I HAVE now taken up my pen to introduce to the notice of the public, a book containing productions of an interesting young authoress. The occasion is one relatively of importance, and certainly of great interest to myself.

I am not in the habit of introducing myself or others to notice by the adjective "colored," &c., but it seems proper that I should just say here, that my authoress is a colored lady, a member of my church, of pleasing piety and modest worth.

The book contains her own thoughts, expressed in her own way. The best way to do justice to young writers, is to weigh their thoughts without so strict a regard to their style as we should pay in the case of elder writers.

The matter of this book is miscellaneous, in *prose* and *poetry*. The topics are judiciously selected, and it must be pleasing to the friends of youthful piety to see that religion is placed first; and the more so when it is known, that in this, the writer has followed her *renewed* turn of mind. The article on religion is full of piety and good sense.

1

This is itself a high commendation to the book. It contains the pious sentiments of a youth devoted to the glory of God, and the best good of her readers. This is an example worthy to be imitated. I know of knothing more praise-worthy than, to see one of such promise come before the public, with the religion of Christ uppermost in her mind. It will be well for our cause when many such can be found among us. In her biographical sketches, she shows in a very interesting way, her *social* piety. She has paid a just tribute to the memory of a number of her departed companions. This has been well conceived. Departed worth deserves permanent tributes. If they were youth, what is more fit than that their surviving youthful companions should pay those tributes?

My authoress has a taste for poetry. And this is much to the advantage of any one who makes an effort in this difficult part of literature. The opinion has too far prevailed, that the talent for poetry is *exclusively* the legacy of nature. Nature should not be charged of withholding her blessings, when the only cause of our barrenness is our own indolence. There is no doubt that the talent for poetry is in a high degree *attainable*. My authoress has evinced her belief in this position. She is willing to be judged by the candid, and even to run the hazard of being severely dealt with by the critic, in order to accomplish something for the credit of her people. She has done well by what nature has done for her, in trying what art will add. The fact is, this is the only way to show the fallacy of that stupid theory, that *nature has done nothing but fit us for slaves, and that art cannot unfit us for slavery!*

My authoress has followed the example of Philis Wheatly, and of Terence, and Capitain, and Francis Williams, her compatriots.

These all served in adversity, and afterwards found that

nature had no *objection*, at least, to their serving the world in high repute as poets. She, like as Philis Wheatly was, is passionately fond of reading, and delights in searching the Holy Scriptures; and is now rapidly improving in knowledge.

Should her book which is here offered, meet with due encouragement, her talents will receive an impetus which will amply repay her patrons, and the generation in which she lives.

To those with whom my authoress is more particularly identified, I must remark, that so far from having a pretence to disparage her book, we have many considerations which enforce the obligation to give it a prompt and ready patronage. To some of these I beg leave to advert, in conclusion.

1. Young writers are always in *peculiar need of patronage* to enable them to set out in a successful and useful career. It is often the case, that their fortune turns upon their first attempt, and that they fail, not so much for want of merit, as for want of that patronage which their merit deserves.

Elder writers, in general, have gained a reputation, and therefore have this acquisition to augment their chance for patronage in any particular effort. But the young writer has no such capital to begin with. In their first effort for patronage the odds is against them, since they have, at the same time, to try for reputation. Under these circumstances they more naturally look to those whose sympathies *ought* to be in favor of their success.

2. From the above general principle, our young authoress justly appeals to *us*, her own people, (though not exclusively,) to give her success. I say the appeal is *just*. And it is just because her success will, relatively, be our own. A mutual effort is the legitimate way to secure

mutual success. Egypt, Greece and Rome, successively, gave their own authors success, and by a very natural consequence, the reputation which they secured to their authors became their own. The history of the arts and sciences is the history of individuals, of individual nations. When Egypt was a school for the world, all the Egyptians were not teachers of the arts and sciences. The Romans were not all Ciceros, nor were the Greeks all Homers, or Platos. But as Greece had a Plato why may we not have a Platoess ?

3. This book has a claim upon our youth, and especially those of the writers own sex. She has a large heart full of chaste and pious affection for those of her own age and sex; and this affection is largly interspersed over the pages of her book. If you will reciprocate this affection you will, I doubt not, read this book with pleasure and profit. With these remarks, and my best wishes to you and our authoress, I close, that you may pass on to her own pages, and read for your improvement.

JAMES W. C. PENNINGTON,

Pastor of the Colored Congregational Church.

HARTFORD, June 1st, 1841.

MISCELLANEOUS PIECES
IN PROSE.

RELIGION.

RELIGION is the daughter of Heaven — parent of our virtues, and source of all true felicity. She alone giveth peace and contentment; divests the heart of anxious cares, bursts on the mind a flood of joy, and sheds unmingled and pretenatural sunshine in the pious breast. By her the spirits of darkness are banished from the earth, and angelic ministers of grace thicken, unseen, the regions of mortality. She promotes love and good will among men — lifts up the head that hangs down — heals the wounded spirit — dissipates the gloom of sorrow — sweetens the cup of affliction — blunts the sting of death, and whatever seen, felt and enjoyed, breathes around her an everlasting spring.

Religion raises men above themselves: irreligion sinks them beneath the brutes. The one makes them angels; the other makes them evil spirits. *This* binds them down to a poor pitiable speck of perishable earth ; *that* opens up a vista to the skies, and lets loose all the principles of an immortal mind, among the glorious objects of an eternal world.

The religion of Christ not only arms us with fortitude against the approach of evil, but supposing evils to fall upon us with the heaviest pressure, it lightens the load by many consolations to which others are strangers. While bad men trace in the calamities with which they are visited, the hand of an offended Sovereign, Christians are taught to view them as well-intended chastisements of a merciful father. They hear, amidst them, that still voice which a good conscience brings to their ear : " Fear not, for I am with thee ; be not dismayed, for I am thy God."

Where can the soul find refuge but in the bosom of religion ? There she is admitted to those prospects of providence and futurity which alone can warm and fill the heart. Lift up thy head, O Christian, and look forward to yon calm, unclouded regions of mercy, unfilled by vapors, unruffled by storms — where celestial friendship, the loveliest form in Heaven, never dies, never changes, never cools ! Soon thou shalt burst this brittle earthly poison of the body, break the fetter of mortality, spring to endless life, and mingle with the skies.

How many of us are able to say that we are persuaded that neither life nor death, nor things present, nor things to to come, nor heighth, nor depth, nor any other creature, shall be able to separate us from the love of God, which is in Christ Jesus, our Lord. Religion confers on the mind principles of noble independence. " The upright man is satisfied from himself;" he despises not the advantages of fortune, but he centers not his happiness in them. With a moderate share of them he can be contented ; and contentment is felicity. Happy in his own integrity, conscious of the esteem of good men, reposing firm trust in providence, and the promises of God, he is exempted from servile dependence on other things. He can wrap himself up in a good conscience, and look forward, without terror, to the change of the world. Let all things fluctuate around him as they please, that by the Divine ordination, they shall be made to work together in the issue, for his good ; and, therefore, having much to hope from God, and little to fear from the world, he can be easy in every state. One who possesses within himself such an establishment of mind, is truly free.

The character of God, as Supreme Ruler of the world, demands our supreme reverence, and our cordial and entire obedience to his will. Hence proceeds our duty to worship him ; for worship, external acts of homage, are the means of preserving, in our minds that fear and reverence, a spirit of obedience. Neglect of worshiping God is inevitably followed by forgetfulness of God, and by consequence, a loss of the reverence for his authority, which prompts to obedience. We know that God is love ; and love among men is the *fulfilment of the law*. Love is the principal source of other virtues, and of all genuine happiness. From a supreme love to God, and from a full persuasion of his perfect benevolence and almighty power, springs *confidence* —a trusting in him for protection, for safety, for support, and for final salvation. This confidence in God, springing from love, implying cordial aprobation of his character, and obedience to his gospel, is *Christian faith.* This is the *anchor of the soul, sure* and *steadfast ;* the foundation of the Christian's hope; it is this alone which sustains the good man amidst all the storms of life, and enables him to meet adversity, in all its forms, with firmness and tranquility.

It is impossible to love God without desiring to please him, and as far as we are able, to resemble him ; therefore, the love of God must lead to every virtue, in the highest degree. We may be sure we do not truly love him, if we content ourselves with avoiding flagrant sins, and not strive, in good earnest, to reach the greatest degree of perfection of which we are capable. Thus do these few words direct us to the highest Christian virtue. Indeed, the whole tenor of the gospel is to offer us every help, direction and motive that can enable us to attain that degree of faith, on which depends our eternal good.

There are many circumstances in our situation that peculiarly require the support of religion to enable us to act in them with spirit and propriety. Our whole life is often a life of suffering. We can not engage in business, or dissipate ourselves·in pleasure and riot as irreligious men too often do : We must bear our sorrows in silence, unknown and unpitied. We must often put on a face of serenity and cheerfulness when our hearts are torn with an-guish, or sinking in despair.

There is not, in my opinion, a more pleasing and triumphant consideration in religion, than this :

of the perpetual progress which the soul makes towards the perfection of its nature, without ever arriving at a period in it. To look upon the soul as going on from strength to strength to consider that she is to shine forever with new accessions of glory, and brighten to all eternity ; that she will be adding virtue to virtue, and knowledge to knowledge ; carries in it something wonderfully agreeable to that ambition which is natural to the mind of man. Nay, it must be pleasing to God himself, to see his creation forever beautifying in his eyes, and drawing nearer to him by greater degrees of resemblance. With what astonishment and veneration may we look into God's own word, where there are such hidden stores of virtue and knowledge, such inexhaustable sources of perfection ! We know not yet what we shall be ; nor has it ever entered into the heart of man to conceive the glory that will be always in reserve for him.

Thus make our lives glide on serenely ; and when the angel of death receives his commission to put a period to our existence, may we receive the summons with tranquility, and pass without fear the gloomy valley which separates time from eternity. May we remember that this life is nothing more than a short duration, a prelude to another, which will never have an end.

Happy thou to whom the present life has no charms for which thou canst wish it to be protracted. Thy troubles will soon vanish like a dream, which mocks the power of memory ; and what signify all the shocks which thy feeling spirit can meet with in this transitory world? A few moments longer, and thy complaints will be forever at an end; thy disease of body and mind shall be felt no more; the ungenerous hints of churlish relations shall distress, fortune frown, and futurity intimidate no more. Then shall thy voice, no longer breathing the plaintive strains of melancholy, but happily attend, attuned to songs of gladness, mingle with the hosts, mortals or immortals sung: "*O, Death! where is thy sting? O, Grave! where is thy victory? Thanks be to God, who giveth us the victory, through our Lord Jesus Christ; — blessing and honor, glory and power, be unto him that sits upon the throne, and unto the Lamb forever and ever.*"

EDUCATION.

THIS appears to be the great source from which nations have become civilized, industrious, respectable and happy. A society or people are always considered as advancing, when they are found paying proper respect to education. The observer will find them erecting buildings for the establishment of schools, in various sections of their country, on different systems, where their children may at an early age commence learning, and having their habits fixed for higher attainments. Too much attention, then, can not be given to it by people, nation, society or individual. History tells us that the first settlers of our country soon made themselves conspicuous by establishing a character for the improvement, and diffusing of knowledge among them.

We hear of their inquiry, how shall our children be educated ? and upon what terms or basis shall it be placed ? We find their questions soon answered to that important part ; and by attending to this in every stage of their advancement, with proper respect, we find them one of the most enlightened and happy nations on the globe.

It is, therefore, an unspeakable blessing to be born in those parts where wisdom and knowledge flourish ; though it must be confessed there are even in these parts several poor, uninstructed persons who are but little above the late inhabitants of this country, who knew no modes of the civilized life, but wandered to and fro, over the parts of the then unknown world.

We are, some of us, very fond of knowledge, and apt to value ourselves upon any proficiency in the sciences ; one science, however, there is, worth more than all the rest, and that is the science of living well — which shall remain " when tongues shall cease," and "knowledge shall vanish away."

It is owing to the preservation of books, that we are led to embrace their contents. Oral instructions can benefit but one age and one set of hearers ; but these silent teachers address all ages and all nations. They may sleep for a while and be neglected ; but whenever the desire of information springs up in the human breast, there they are with mild wisdom ready to instruct and please us.

No person can be considered as possessing a good education without religion. A good education is that which prepares us for our future sphere of action and makes us contented with that situation in life in which God, in his infinite mercy, has seen fit to place us, to be perfectly resigned to our lot in life, whatever it may be. Religion has been decreed as the passion of weak persons ; but the Bible tells us " to seek first the kingdom of heaven, and His righteousness, and all other things shall be added unto us." This world is only a place to prepare for another and a better.

If it were not for education, how would our heathen be taught therefrom ? While science and the arts boast so many illustrious names ; there is another and more extended sphere of action where illustrious names and individual effort has been exerted with the happiest results, and their authors, by their deeds of charity, have won bright and imperishable crowns in the realms of bliss. Was it the united effort of nations, or of priestly synods that first sent the oracles of eternal truth to the inhospitable shores of Greenland — or placed the lamp of life in the hut of the Esquemaux — or carried a message of love to the burning climes of Africa — or that directed the deluded votaries of idolatry in that benighted land where the Ganges rolls its consecrated waters, to Calvary's Sacrifice, a sacrifice that sprinkled with blood the throne of justice, rendering it accessible to ruined, degraded man.

In proportion to the education of a nation, it is rich and powerful. To behold the wealth and power of Great Britain, and compare it with China ; America with Mexico ; how confused are the ideas of the latter, how narrow their conceptions, and are, as it were in an unknown world.

Education is a system which the bravest men have followed. What said Alexander about this? Said he : "I am more indebted to my tutor, Aristotle, than to my father Philip ; for Philip gives me my living, but Aristotle teaches me how to live." It was Newton that threw aside the dimness of uncertainty which shrouded for so many centuries the science of astronomy ; penetrated the arena of nature, and soared in his eagle-flight far, far beyond the wildest dreams of all former ages, defining with certainty the motions of those flaming worlds, and assigning laws to the fartherest star that lies on the confines of creation — that glimmers on the verge of immensity.

Knowledge is the very foundation of wealth, and of nations. Aristotle held unlimited control over the opinions of men for fifteen centuries, and governed the empire of mind where ever he was known. For knowledge, men brave every danger, they explore the sandy regions of Africa, and diminish the arena of contention and bloodshed. Where ever ignorance holds unlimited sway, the light of science, and the splendor of the gospel of truth is obscure and nearly obliterated by the gloom of monkish superstition, merged in the sable hues of idolatry and popish cruelty ; no ray of glory shines on those degraded minds ; "darkness covers the earth, and gross darkness the people."

Man is the noblest work in the universe of God. His excellence does not consist in the beautiful symmetry of his form, or in the exquisite structure of his complicated physical machinery ; capable of intellectual and moral powers. What have been the conquests of men in the field of general science ? What scholastic intrenchment is there which man would not have wished to carry — what height is there which he would not have wished to survey — what depth that he would not like to explore ? — even the mountains and the earth — hidden minerals — and all that rest on the borders of creation he would like to overpower.

But shall these splendid conquests be subverted ? Egypt, that once shot over the world brilliant rays of genius, is sunk in darkness. The dust of ages sleeps on the besom of Roman warriors, poets, and orators. The glory of Greece has departed, and leaves no Demosthenes to thunder with his eloquence, or Homer to soar and sing.

It is certainly true that many dull and unpromising scholars have become the most distinguished men ; as Milton, Newton, Walter Scott, Adam Clarke. Newton stated of himself, that his superiority to common minds was not natural, but acquired by mental discipline. Hence, we perceive that the mind is capable of wonderful improvement. The mother of Sir William Jones said to to him when a child : " If you wish to understand, read ;" how true, that " education forms the mind."

How altogether important, then, is education ; it is our guide in youth, and it will walk with us in the vale of our declining years. This knowledge we ought ever to pursue with all dillgence. Our whole life is but one great school ; from the

cradle to the grave we are all learners ; nor will our education be finished until we die.

A good education is another name for happiness. Shall we not devote time and toil to learn how to be happy ? It is a science which the youngest child may begin, and the wisest man is never weary of. No one should be satisfied with present attainments ; we should aim high, and bend all our energies to reach the point aimed at.

We ought not to fail to combine with our clear convictions of what is right, a firmness and moral courage sufficient to enable us to " forsake every false way," and our course will be like that of the just — " brighter and brighter unto the perfect day."

BENEVOLENCE.

Youth is the proper season for cultivating the benevolent and humane affections. As a great part of your happiness is to depend on the connections which you may form with others, it is of high importance that you acquire betimes the temper and the manners which will render such connections comfortable. May a sense of justice be the foundation of all your social qualities. In your most early intercourse with the world, and even in

2

your youthful amusements, may no unfeelingness be found. Engrave on your minds the sacred rule of "doing unto others as you would wish them to do unto you." For this end, impress yourselves with a deep sense of the original and natural equality of men.

True benevolence ought to reign in every person; it does not shut our eyes to the distinction between good and bad persons, or between one nation and another, or between two stations; or to warm the heart unequally to those who befriend us, and those who injure us. It reserves our esteem for good and bad men, and our complacency for our friends.

Towards our enemies it inspires forgiveness, humanity, and a solicitude for their welfare. It breathes universal candor, and liberality of sentiment. It forms gentleness of temper, and dictates affability of manners. If human understanding apprehends any thing according to truth and right, the *benevolent* character is the proper object of the love of every rational mind, as the contrary is the natural object of aversion. Every human, or other finite mind, is more or less amiable, according as it has more or less of this excellent disposition; it is evident that infinite goodness is infinitely amiable.

True benevolence and humility are always acceptable, and always knows. We ought not to do any thing benevolently, from vanity, or a desire of having our deeds known or applauded. Strive to remember those benevolent and immortal men who have done so much good in our country, and are still doing, and perhaps will not stop until death shall have put an end to their labors, and their works.

Think of the benevolent and immortal John Howard, putting pleasure far from him, to the intention of promoting good. John Elliot devoted his days to the instruction of the poor Indians. And ever regardless of his own wants, supplied others, and neglected himself.

We ought not one of us ever to be weary in well doing. But feel, and esteem it necessary for us to do good, in what shape soever it calls upon us. It is the duty of the young, as well as those who are grown up, to study the best means of relieving the destitute.

To remove ignorance is an important branch of benevolence. To distribute or lend useful, and religious books, is an important branch of benevolence. For what is better than instructing the mind: it is certainly better than giving money or clothes, which soon pass away, and may be misused.

I have known Ladies forming themselves into a society, for the purpose of assisting the poor ; and have done much good in the undertaking. The young should always solicit the advice of their parents, or older friends, in their charities; for they may bestow charity without consideration. The relief of the poor require more knowledge of mankind, than those whose years are few, can be expected to possess.

There was a gentleman, who was esteemed high in the Courts of our land, who was rich in posses-sions, yet refused an aged, and tattered beggar, who asked alms of him. Said he, " if I had authority, I would put you, and all such others into close custody. Begone from my doors, I will not give you a farthing."

I should think this very improper, and very unnatural for a person to say who was not wealthy, much more, for a person who has a plenty of this world's goods, and professes Christianity. I ask any one, "hoarded up, what is wealth?" It certainly can afford no real comfort to themselves, or others.

Says a writer, "Integrity, or the observance of justice, then, is essential to private and public happiness. It is the fundamental principle in all the numerous concerns of society. Every deviation from justice and rectitude among men, is a violation of the divine commands."

It is beautifully observed by a British author, that, "there is happiness in the very wish to make others happy." It is thus that the pleasures derived from good actions comes in aid of moral precepts. We are excited by our own happiness to do what conscience dictates, and the laws of God require. In all cases of this kind, our happiness coincides with our duty. And it is thus that man becomes a miniature likeness of his Maker, in whom are inseparably united supreme moral excellence and supreme felicity !

Let not ease and indulgence contract our affections, and wrap us up in selfish enjoyment. Let us ever accustom ourselves to think of the distresses of human life : of the solitary cottage, the dying parent, and the weeping orphan. Never sport with pain or distress in any amusement, nor treat even the meanest insect with wanton cruelty.

DILIGENCE AND NEGLIGENCE.

A BABE slept in its cradle, and its name was Diligence. It was joyful in the hands of those who nursed it. It was healthful, and ever playful, waiting for the fond caress of its parents. It bid fair promise to become a man.

The babe grew to be a boy. Among the thoughts which visit children, came one whose name was Negligence. It came to him with pretended diligence, and tried to enforce upon him the name of Negligence. The parents said to Diligence, "remove this Negligence far from you." But Negligence said, "trust in me, and I will tell thee of what thou hast not seen."

"And of what canst thou tell me," replied Diligence. Then answered Negligence, "Diligence is an unknown path, and o'er scattered by many thorns. Where none that are wise do ever travel, and which, in the end, will cause you much trouble."

"I will not listen to thy idle tale," said he, "depart from me, I know you not, or from whence you are. I have often heard said that you depart from the right course, merely for making your way easier. But I will have naught to do, or say to you; I will try to walk in the path which my fathers have walked in before me."

The boy became a youth. Once, as he lay in his bed, Diligence and Negligence came to his pillow. Negligence was merry, and talked easy of life. And said he, " follow me, and be regardless of habit, and thy heart shall be merry as mine, when I sing to thee."

But Diligence said, " youth, be mine altogether ; for Diligence and Negligence cannot remain together. Diligence is not slow to perseverence, is active in duty, and will be a friend to *him* all his life long."

When he awoke, Negligence had left him, but Diligence staid to bless him. He became a man, but Diligence was constant with him. And he drank deep at the fountains of Intelligence.

At length, age found the man, and turned the hairs of his head white. His eye grew dim, and the world seemed to him an altered place. But, Alas ! he had changed, and the blood was now cold in his veins.

Diligence looked on him and spoke to him in graver tones than in former times, and was to him a long tried friend. He sat down beside him, and the aged man said, " Diligence, thou hast been with me. Thou hast staid me, and improved my intellect, which might have been lost."

Then answered Diligence meekly, " It may be so. I trust that all who follow this principle, may never disown their name. I have borne it for years, and am not yet tired. I have lost none of the precepts which its gems afforded, they are as brilliant as when they first came into my hands."

Negligence looked mournful, and ceased to ask to be forgiven of her error. She stopped in her career, and was no more to go forth, singing naught but merry songs all the days of her life.

The old man laid down to die. "His spirit ascended to God who gave it." Diligence tarried with him till the last; but Negligence fled before the time.

A glorious form bent o'er the dying man, whose name was Religion. It wept over him, and his friend, commended them to future happiness. For said Religion, " Thou has been faithful over a few things, Christ will make thee ruler over many things. Enter thou into the joy of thy Lord."

TWO SCHOOL GIRLS.

I heard two girls as they conversed. " Good morning," said one, " where are you walking, and don't you calculate to attend school any more ?" The answer was, "I am going to visit our Natural History Room; and do not think of attending school at present."

With these two girls I was well acquainted. Afterwards, as I reflected, I could not help saying to myself, " I think by her appearance in school, that she does not gain as much useful knowledge, as the one who was about to visit the Natural History Room."

In school, she does not pay that attention to

studies as does her friend. She hastily runs over them, and pursues the lessons that require the least labor. Gives a short recitation of poetry and dialogue. She undertakes mathematics, and thinks them too dull for her — at length they are dropped. Her writing is ill performed. Her rapid and confused elocution, if not attended too, will be found adhesive through life. On this account her teacher is often obliged to speak to her, while at recitation.

Her friend is an industrious and careful girl while in school. She seeks knowledge from the most difficult and useful studies, as well as those which are less so. She collects her mind and thoughts upon the lesson which may be marked for her.

Although not in school as much as the other, still she has gained more useful knowledge, and is more prepared to encounter the world's troubles. She who is not willing to contend with difficulties, is not fitted for this world. " The being who best knows for what end we were placed here, has scattered in our path something beside roses."

Although she was not altogether distinguished for fine talents, yet she was a thorough scholar. Her answers were with entire correctness and precision. When not in school, she employed herself in that which would give her the most useful and solid instruction. She visited scenes which would help to deepen that knowledge.

She felt strongly, that strength of intellect is acquired by conquering hard studies, and strength of character by overcoming obstacles. She knew that knowledge painfully gained was not easily lost.

Look at them, after their course of scholastic training! One, with her family, considering it her ambition to make a showy appearance. No rational economy — no patience to study, nor self-control to practice. By her wasteful expenditure of dress, and servants, their affairs became seriously embarrassed; and she too helpless to do anything in their distress.

The fortune of the husband of her friend was not large; but by constant economy, she was able to secure every comfort, and to remember the poor. Her family was well regulated, and taught order, industry, and perseverance which she herself had learned. In observing these families, it was clear whose was the seat of the greatest order, comfort and happiness.

"Time was, when the temple of science was barred against the foot of woman. Heathen tyranny held her in vassalage, and Mahometan prejudice pronounced her without a soul. Now, from the sanctuary which knowledge and wisdom have consecrated, and from whence she was so long excluded, the interdict is taken away. How does she prize the gift? Does she press to gain a stand at the temple of knowledge, or will she clothe her brow in vanity, and be satisfied with ignorance. May we improve the influence which is now given us, and seek for " glory and immortality beyond the grave."

DECISION OF CHARACTER.

DECISION means determination. Where a person is decided in a point, we say that he has come to a full determination. Those who wish to be useful members of society, must come to decided opinions. Such persons are most useful in the domestic circle, and the most useful in community.

To be diligent in any one thing, it requires that you should be decided. You cannot be diligent in your studies, without coming to the decision that you will be so. Columbus would not have discovered America had he not come to the determination that he would seek for a far distant country.

Amidst all difficulties, Columbus displayed those traits of character which proved the greatness of his mind, and his peculiar fitness for the arduous duties of his station. He appeared with a steady and cheerful countenance, as satisfied with what he had done. He soothed his companions by holding out to them a prospect of riches and of fame, and by offering a gratuity to him who should first discover land.

Having fully made up his mind to seek another country, he underwent all the threats and cruel treatment of his companions. After having undergone the siege of the first discovery, it was given the name of America, in honor of a Florentine Nobleman, named Americus Vespucius.

Think of the decision of Demosthenes; his

elocution was so incorrect, that he could not pronounce some letters; and he was so short breathed that he could not utter a whole period without stopping. He at length overcame all these obstacles, to the surprise of the nation. Cicero tells us that his success was so great that all Greece came in crowds to Athens to hear him speak; and he was said to be a distinguished orator.

In some of the decided examples of ambition, we almost revere the force of mind which impelled them forward through the longest series of action, superior to doubt and fluctuation, and disdainful of ease, of pleasure, of opposition, and of hazard.

We bow to the ambitious spirit which reached the true sublime in the reply of Pompey, a distinguished Roman General, to his friends, who dissuaded him from venturing on a tempestuous sea, in order to be at Rome on an important occasion: "It is necessary for me to go — it is necessary for me to live."

"A little ship, floating on the stream, is tossed here and there by every little breeze and wave, while the huge log ploughs its course majestically along, undisturbed by the raging winds or foaming billows. The former represents the undecided man, the latter the decided man."

The lightning, as it flashes from cloud to cloud, or plays around the metallic rod, immortalizes the decision of Franklin; the comprehensive mind of Fulton grasped an object considered hitherto unattainable; and, by his happy application of a most stupendous power, he has triumphed o'er the winds, conquered the elements, annihilated space, extended the bounds of social intercourse; thus cementing the bounds of union between distant nations. Even now, the swift heralds of his fame are dashing through the foaming billows, bearing the spirit of enterprize from the Thames to the Mediterranean, from the blue waters of the Hudson to where Euphrates rolls its silver flood.

After Robert Bruce had been defeated twelve times, as he lay on some straw in a barn, brooding over his misfortunes, and on the point of giving up in despair, he beheld a spider attempt in vain twelve times to ascend the beam, but its thirteenth attempt was crowned with success. He then arose, and determined to make one more vigorous effort in the cause of liberty; he did so, and it was crowned with equal success. The use of decision will raise you to elevated stations — its neglect will sink you to ruin.

THE SEASONS.

In contemplating on the various scenes of life, the vicissitudes of the seasons, the perfect regularity, order, and harmony of nature, we cannot but be filled with wonder and admiration, at the consummate wisdom and benificence of the all wise and gracious Creator. His consummate wisdom and goodness have made the various seasons of the year perfectly consonant to the refined feelings of man, and peculiarly adapted them to the universal preservation of nature.

We say to spring, " dreary winter is passed ; its severe cold is mitigated ; the returning zephyrs dissolve the fleecy snow, and unlock the frozen streams, which overflow the extensive meadows, and enrich the teeming earth. The rapid streams begin to glide gently within their banks ; the spacious meadows soon receive their usual verdure, and the whole face of nature assumes a cheerful aspect. By the refreshing showers, and vivifying powers of the genial sun, we behold the rapid and amazing progress of vegetation."

In summer, men travel about, they wander wide in pursuit of pleasure. Under the burning suns of summer, the farmer works and is wearied. The short nights scarcely refresh him, after the labor of the long days. Summer brings flowers, and permits us to admire nature's works. During the mild seasons, the father prepares what is necessary in his family for winter; the mother calculates garments for her little ones, to shield them from the inclemency of that approaching season.

In autumn, the farmer hastens to the field, to gather his crops. And it is autumn that brings us fruit, and repays us for the toils of summer. The leaves fall from the trees, flowers begin to fade, and die ! This is a good period of the year to contemplate the shortness of life ; and like the autumn, our bodies must decay and turn to dust.

In winter, nature enjoys repose. The trees cease from putting forth leaves, and the plants lay their sweet heads in their bed, the cradle of snow. In winter the students gain much time for meditation; and winter knowledge strikes a deeper root into the mind. It is the season that the child sees more of its father. The laborer gains strength for the ensuing summer. It is then the time to assist the poor, and show pity and kindness to the sick.

May the contemplation of the seasons, lead our minds to a great and glorious God, " the giver of every good and perfect gift." So shall these seasons be remembered in that world where no ice binds the sweet stream, and where there is neither storm nor tempest.

OBEDIENCE.

OBEDIENCE to parents is the BASIS of all order and improvement, and is not only pre-emptorily and repeatedly enjoined by Scripture, but even the heathen laid great stress upon the due performance of obedience to parents and other superiors. The young rose up and gave place to them. They solicited their opinion, and listened attentively until they had done speaking. They bowed down reverently before them, and sought opinions of their hoary men; and withheld not the reverence from them that was their due.

We read, indeed, that the Romans gave to parents unlimited jurisdiction over their children ; and fathers were empowered to (and frequently did) punish filial disobedience with *stripes, slavery,* and even DEATH. "Honor thy father and thy mother, that thy days may be long on the land which the Lord thy God giveth thee," is the solemn command of the MOST HIGH ; and we may safely assure ourselves that God will not only bless the dutiful here, and hereafter, but that he will punish, in the most signal and terrible manner, all those who, by parental neglect and unfilial conduct, set at defiance his written law, and violate that holy and just principle which he has implanted in every human breast.

Youth, in particular, should constantly bear in mind, that every comfort they enjoy, all the intellectual attainments which render them superior to the savage, they owe to their parents. Think of the miseries of orphanage. The greatest loss that can befall a child, is to be deprived of pious and affectionate parents. While you are surrounded by such blessings, never be so ungrateful as to injure them by disobedience.

In their absence, their commands ought always to be observed the same as in their presence. To obey willingly, is a love of obedience. Who would not doubt the obedience of a child, when told by his superior to do as he was bid ; when some minutes after, to be asked, if he had done as he was bade ? I should doubt its obedience when I heard the command.

It is a great duty of the young to treat old persons with respect. The Bible commands them

" to rise up before the face of the old man, and to honor the hoary head." This is too often forgotten, although a command from the Bible. You remember the scenes of a hoary headed man, while in an assembly at Athens, but again in Sparta, he was in a similar situation, but was treated with respect. " The Athenians KNOW what is right," said he, " but the Spartans PRACTICE it."

May it never be said of us, that we understand our duties, yet fail in regarding them. In walking I have often observed a want of reverence which is due to the aged. Years have given them experience which is worthy of honor. If the Bible were not disregarded in this, they would at once receive the respect which is due to them. If in nations the laws are disregarded, what safety is there for the people ?

When you are in school, consider it a privilege to be there, and give your time and thought to the employment which is marked for you, by your teacher. Those who think thus will keep all the rules, and consider it improper to break them. If pupils refuse to obey the directions of their teacher, no benefit can be received from their instructions.

If persons know not obedience how can they teach it to others, which may in time be their lot? A person who will not obey, is not capable of commanding obedience. They know not how to estimate a duty so valuable. Those who are distinguished by faithfully discharging their first and earliest obligations, will be prepared to act well their part in future life. They will maintain good order in their own families, and honor just government in the land.

It is, however, certain, that in whatever situation of life a person is placed in, from the cradle to the grave, a spirit of obedience and submission, pliability of temper, and humility of mind, are required from them ; and the most highly gifted cannot pass over it, without injury to their character.   Let us ever live with principles of obedience ; and that with us we may carry it to our graves ; and when we lay upon our beds of death, may we say to the living — live with this great duty — Obedience.

EMPLOYMENT OF TIME

To MAKE a good use of time, each minute must be well spent.   It is well said, by a celebrated author, that many persons lose two or three hours every day for the want of employing odd minutes. A certain regularity is absolutely necessary, to make a proper use of time.

In the distribution of your time, let the first hour of the day be devoted to the service of God. Accustom yourselves to the practice of religious duties, as a natural expression of gratitude to HIM for all his bounty and benevolence.   Consider it as the service of the God of your fathers ; of HIM to whom your parents devoted you ; of HIM whom, in former ages, your ancestors honored, and by whom they are now rewarded and blessed in heaven.

Time to you is every thing, if well improved. " Time," said Dr. Franklin, " is money." An Italian Philosopher said that " time was his estate." In employing your time, consider it your privilege to spend your leisure hours in deepening the mind, and preparing yourselves for future action.

The human mind was made for action. In virtuous action consists its highest enjoyment. Reading is good employment, and very useful, if well understood. Some books are injurious to the mind, as well as useful. Books have a silent, but powerful influence in the formation of character. Says a distinguished clergyman, " let me see the private books of an individual, and I will tell you his character." Says another, " let me write the private books of a nation, and I care not who makes the laws."

The poems of Homer inspired Alexander with an insatiable thirst for fame and military glory, and they were the foundation of the superstructure that covered the world. The memoirs of this conqueror stamped a like character upon Cæsar ; these, and similar ones, made Napoleon a second Alexander.

Whatever you pretend to learn, be sure and have ambition enough to desire to excel in ; for mediocrity is a proof of weakness ; and perfection may always be purchased by application. " Knowledge," says an elegant writer, " is a comfortable and necessary shelter for us in an advanced age ;" but if you do not plant it while young it will afford you no shade when you become old.

To instruct others is beneficial to the mind. It deepens the knowledge which it already possesses, and quickens it to acquire more. It is beneficial to the moral habits. It teaches self-control. It moves to set a good example. It improves the affections. For we love those whom we make wiser and better, and their gratitude is a sweet reward.

Time is more valuable than money. If you hinder a scholar from studying, you commit a robbery against him ; for robbers of time, are more guilty, than robbers of money. The young are not apt to value the importance of time. They forget that time is money ! If time was more improved, there would be more happiness, and less discontentment, than there is at this present date.

Perhaps many consider that their station in life is too high, to admit of having employment. I think some will say that none are in too high station, be their knowledge ever so deep, to make a proper use of time.

When the unfortunate Greeks stood in need of assistance, ladies of the greatest wealth, plied their needles industriously that the unfortunate people might be clothed. Their servants also came offering a part of their wages. They sat down by their side, working for the same charity ; while the young ones said to each other, " Greece hungered, and we gave her food ; she was naked, and we clothed her."

May we not rest in our beds until we have made

up our minds to ask God for assistance, in making a proper use of time. It will be for our edification, and for memorable thoughts, in our declining years of life.

―――――――――――――――――

EMINENCE FROM OBSCURITY.

MANY instances are known of obscure youths becoming the most distinguished men. There are not the number in this country, who have passed through so many hidden difficulties, and have overcome the like obstacles, as in the Mother Country.

Perhaps you have seen the son of the rich man, expensively dressed, having many attendants, and exercising all the pomp and magnificence, which worldly riches can give. You say in your heart, HOW HAPPY the MAN! He may be, and he may not be. This depends upon the state of matters within. As to knowledge, they may say, I have plenty of time for it, my father is rich in possessions, and I have naught to disturb me from learning, when I choose.

But this is not the case with the poor. They are compelled to practice industry. This protects them from many vices and promotes health, and self-approbation.

If their object is to attain an education, and they

are obliged to be partially occupied in those toils by which subsistance is gained, of course, they will value more highly, every fragment of time, than those whose leisure is uninterrupted. A sense of the value of time, is one of the first steps, which some have made in improvement and wisdom.

Another privilege, is the habit of overcoming obstacles. Strength of mind, and moral energy, are thus acquired. Those who lead lives of indulgence, have not the opportunity of learning that perseverance " which is daunted by no difficulty, and without which genius avails little."

Distinction is sometimes gained by those who rise from obscure birth, by viewing the contrast. The fame of Dr .Franklin, is heightened by the circumstance, that he was a printer's boy, and the son of a chandler ; and that of Bently, the celebrated English scholar, by the fact, that he was the son of a blacksmith.

Bloomfield, the poet, was the son of a tailor, and an apprentice to a shoemaker. He was busily employed at his trade, while composing the " Farmer's Boy," and being often destitute of paper, retained great numbers of his lines in memory, until he could obtain materials, and time for writing.

Inigo Jones, the great architect, was the son of a cloth-manufacturer, and it was intended that he should be a mechanic. Sir Edmund Saunders, chief justice, in the reign of Charles the Second, was an errand boy.

Winckelman, a distinguished writer on classical antiquities, and the fine arts, was the son of a shoemaker. He supported himself while at college, chiefly by teaching younger students, and at the same time, aided in maintaining his poor, sickly father.

The celebrated Metastasio, was the son of a poor mechanic. The father of Opie, a distinguished portrait painter, was a carpenter ; and he, himself was raised from the bottom of a saw-pit where he labored as a wood-cutter, to the professorship of painting, in the Royal Academy, at London.

The learned Dr. Prideaux, bishop of Worcester, obtained his education, by walking on foot, to Oxford, and getting employment, at first, as assistant in the kitchen of Exeter College.

Haydn, the celebrated musical composer, was the son of a wheel-wright, who officated also as sexton ; and his mother, was a servant in the family of a neighboring nobleman.

Dr. Isaac Milnor, who filled the chair as Professor of Mathematics, at Cambridge, which Sir Isaac Newton occupied, was once a weaver ; as was also his brother, the author of the well known Church History.

Dr. White, professor of Arabic, in the University of Oxford, England, was originally, a weaver : and James Ferguson, the celebrated writer on Astronomy, was the son of a day-laborer.

Having discovered, when quite a child, some important truths in mechanics, he went on to illustrate them, without teacher or book and with no other tools, than a little knife and a simple turning lathe.

While in the employment of a farmer, he improved every slight interval of leisure in constructing models, during the day, and studying the stars at night. He was elected a member of the Royal

Society, and King George, the third, after hearing his lectures, settled on him an annual pension; while his writing still continue the admiration of the men of science.

The celebrated Benjamin Johnson worked as a bricklayer and a mason. Thomas Sympson, an able English scholar, Professor of Mathematics, and Fellow of the Royal Society, was the son of a weaver. Castalio, who translated the Bible into Latin, was the son of poor peasants, and reared by them, in the midst of privations, among the mountains of Dauphiny. Avaigio, one of the Italian poets, of the sixteenth century, though working with his father, at the trade of a black-smith, till he was eighteen years old, found means to cultivate his genius, and to obtain learning.

Those who have risen from humble stations, often recur with satisfaction to the steps through which they have been led on their upward way. It was pleasing to Aurelian, to have it known that he was the son of peasants. Dioclesian felt that the splendor of his sway in Rome was heightened by his obscure birth, of Dalmatia.

I have now succeeded in telling that eminence has risen from obscurity. Remembering the difficulties which they passed through, they were naturally skilful, patient guides, and qualified to impart somewhat of the perseverance and moral energy which they themselves profited.

If the poor obtain distinguished stations, their sympathies ought to be more active, more over-flowing than those of other men. They must know how to enter the feelings of the humbler classes of society, and to relieve, and take part in their sorrows.

Dear youth of my country, her pride and her hope, catch the spirit of well done Philanthropy. If you cannot surpass the great and the good who have gone before you, study their excellences, walk in their footsteps, and God give you grace to fill their places well, when they are mouldering into dust.

~~~~~~~~~~~~~~~~~~~~~~~~

LESSONS FROM NATURE.

WHEN I was a child, I had great esteem and affection for an aged sire. Years had brought him wisdom, and he was kind as well as wise. So I loved him, and rejoiced much when I saw him coming towards me.

Once, as he talked with me, he said, " have you learned the lessons from nature?" I replied, that his meaning I understood not. Then said he, " Await here on the morrow, and I will hither come ; if that Almighty Being should spare our lives," said he, pointing his hand upward, " thou mayest doat upon our meeting."

On the morrow I went forth, and looked for his coming. At last, I heard a voice speaking unto me, saying, " child, come hither." I turned about and saw the aged man coming towards me, so I ran with joy to meet him.

Said he, "seat thyself down beside me, and listen attentively to all that I shall say. You say that you know naught of nature. What can be more delightful to the human eye than the broad and open field. We can look attentively upon all that passes around. We can look forth, and behold the brooks flowing on among sweet flowers ; observe the grass that grows, the birds that fly high in the air ; they soar aloft, and at last they alight upon the ground.

"The ducklings swim beside their mother in the clear stream — the hen gathers her chickens under her wings to shelter them from harm ; we cast our eyes on yonder pole, and behold the spider throwing out her silvery threads from spray to spray, and the bee hastening to her hive ; the ant carrying in grain for the approaching winter ; to them that admire the works of nature, the fields lift up their hands and cry unto them, " industry is happiness, and idleness is an offence both to nature and to her God."

When he questioned me of knowledge, I confessed that I knew naught of knowledge, save that which I learned of the violets that grew, and the lilly which appears from the vale, and the vines which clime my father's bowers. I was ashamed, and felt that I had need to be taught of nature ; and I yet wished to turn from the wild scenery around, and look into the moral and intellectual views of mankind.

"After I have told thee this much, thou must learn the rest for thyself," said he. "Go at the beautiful dawning of the sun, and when I visit thee again, tell me what thou hast seen."

At length he came; I commenced to tell him what I had seen. "I went forth, and looked attentively upon all that moved around. But no voice spake to me, and no eye regarded me. At dusk, when the evening dews were lingering upon the grass, I saw children who had played with me upon the summer turf. They, too, were untaught, unfed, and they spoke loudly, with unpleasant tongues.

"I asked them why they walked not in the pleasant path of knowledge. And they mocked at me. I said, these souls have the gift of reason, and are born to die; but they spoke more loudly, and seemed to say, ' what seek you among us ? ' "

"I saw the babe that had received its last caress from its mother, the youth that seemed worn down by care, the strong man that was reared like the Oak among trees, the hoary man, that tottered like the babe, bidding a last farewell to the world. The mourners stood by, and me - thought that they soon would be no more.

"I saw a widow standing near an open grave ; her children stood beside her, and were mourning. The widow looked as if naught, save death, would give her relief; yet, I dreampt not of her sorrow. I spake unto her, but she was silent. At last I said, what have made mothers forget their children, and not pity them when they hunger ? What makes friends forget their early love, the youth to lay low in the dust, the beautiful infant to be committed to the grave ? I heard a still small voice saying unto me, 'Disregard to my laws, and for this reason, there is lamentation.' I sighed, and said no more.

" On my way I saw a youth, sitting by the road side, I asked him why he wept ? He replied, ' Because all that was dear to me have fallen in battle.' Said I, tell me of battle ! He answered, ' thou can'st not bear the thought.' Then I entreated him to tell me what he had seen.

" I came," he said, " at the close of day, when the cannons ceased their thunder, and the victor and vanquished had withdrawn. The rising moon looked down upon the pale faces of the dead. Scattered o'er the plain were many who still struggled with the pangs of death.

" They stretched out the shattered limb, yet there was no healing hand. They strove to raise their heads, but sank deeper in the blood which flowed from their own bosoms. They begged, in God's name, that we would put them out of their misery, and their piercing shrieks entered into my soul.

" Here and there horses, mad with pain, rolled and plunged, mangling with their hoofs, the dying, or defacing the dead. Then I remembered the mourners who were left at home." Ere he had finished, I said, ' tell me no more of battle or of war, for I am sick to heart.' He then arose, and I went onward.

I beheld a school house of white. The children stood like lambs before their teachers ; they bowed their ears to instruction, they walked in the paths of knowledge, they were simple and single hearted, and followers of the truth. Sometimes they wept, and again they rejoiced, when none knew why. When I looked upon them, I remembered that our Saviour " took little children in his arms and blessed them."

Then answered this aged sire, "of nature thou ast indeed seen much. Treasure it in thy memory, henceforth, never to be eradicated. We are all God's family, and he provides for all. Although the re are many nations, and many stations in life, yet he watches over us, he has given us immortal souls. Some have white complexions, some are red, like our wandering natives, others have sable or olive complexions." "But God hath made of one blood all who dwell upon the face of the earth."

"They inhabit different climes; some a burning, some a frozen, and others a more temperate climate, but the same sun gives them warmth, the same cloud sends down rain to refresh them. Some press the liquor from the grape, some drink the juice from the palm treé, and many refresh themselves at the fountains of pure water.

"Some slumber on land, in their peaceful and quiet homes; and some upon the tossing treacherous sea. Yet God provides for all. Let us think of our fellow creatures, as under the care of that Merciful Parent, from whom all blessings proceed, and let our good deeds to those who are less fortunate than ourselves, have root in love."

DESCRIPTION OF A DESERT.

"THEY wandered in the wilderness in a solitary way. Thirsty, their souls fainted in them." — PSALMS.

It is difficult to form a correct idea of a desert, without having seen one. It is a vast plain of sands and stones, interspersed with mountains of various sizes and heights, without roads or shelters. They sometimes have springs of water, which burst forth, and create verdant spots.

The most remarkable of deserts is the Sahara. This is a vast plain, but little elevated above the level of the ocean, and covered with sand and gravel, with a mixture of sea shells, and appears like the basin of an evaporated sea.

Amid the desert there are springs of water, which burst forth and create verdant spots, called Oases. There are thirty-two of these which contain fountains, and Date and Palm trees ; twenty of them are inhabited. They serve as stopping places for the caravans, and often contain villages.

Were it not for these no human being could cross this waste of burning sand. So violent, sometimes, is the burning wind, that the scorching heat dries up the water of these springs, and then frequently, the most disastrous consequences follow.

In 1805, a caravan, consisting of 2,000 persons and 1,800 camels, not finding water at the usual resting place, died of thirst, both men and animals. Storms of wind are more terrible on this desert than on the ocean. Vast serges and clouds of red sand are raised and rolled forward, burying every thing in its way, and it is said that whole tribes have thus been swallowed up.

The situation of such is dreadful, and admits of no resource. Many perish victims of the most horrible thirst. It is then that the value of a cup of water is really felt.

" In such a case there is no distinction. If the master has not, the servant will not give it to him ; for very few are the instances where a man will voluntarily lose his life to save that of another. What a situation for a man, though a rich one, perhaps the owner of all the caravan ! He is dying for a cup of water — no one gives it to him ; he offers all he possesses — no one hears him ; they are all dying, though by walking a few hours further, they might be saved.

" In short, to be thirsty in a desert, without water, exposed to the burning sun, without shelter, is the most terrible situation that a man can be placed in, and one of the greatest sufferings that a human being can sustain ; the tongue and lips swell ; a hollow sound is heard in the ears, which brings on deafness, and the brain appears to grow thick and inflamed.

" If, unfortunately, any one falls sick on the road, he must either endure the fatigue of travelling on a camel, (which is troublesome even to healthy people,) or he must be left behind on the sand, without any assistance, and remain so till a slow death come to relieve him. No one remains with him.

not even his old and faithful servant ; no one will stay and die with him ; all pity his fate, but no one will be his companion."

RESIDENCE IN THE COUNTRY.

No SITUATION in life is so favorable to established habits of virtue, and to powerful sentiments of devotion, as a residence in the country, and rural occupations."

The great pursuit of man is after happiness ; it is the first and strongest desire of his nature ; — in every stage of his life he searchers for it as for hid treasures ; courts it under a thousand different shapes ; and, though perpetually disappointed — still persists — runs after and inquires for it afresh — asks every passenger who comes in his way, "Who will show him any good ;"— who will assist him in the attainment of it, or direct him to the discovery of this great end of all his wishes?

" No man, one would think ; would feel so sensible his immediate dependence upon God, as the farmer. For all his peculiar blessings he is invited to look immediately to the bounty of heaven. No secondary cause stands between him and his Maker. To him are essential the regular succession of the seasons, and the timely fall of the rains,

the genial warmth of the sun, the sure produc-
tiveness of the soil, and the certain operations of
those laws of nature, which must appear to him
nothing less than the varied exertions of Omni-
present energy."

I once passed several weeks in the family of a
farmer. It was one of the most pleasant, and useful visits I ever had made. I ever saw, that industry, contentment, and economy which constitutes
every happy household.

The whole family rose before the sun. Before
eating breakfast, the farmer commended himself,
and his family to the care of God through the day.
When breakfast was over, every one proceeded to
the regular business of the day. The farmer with
his sons, and workmen went to the field. The
mother and daughters took their stand to superin-
tend the household affairs.

When I looked about the house, and saw the
many comforts of the family, and that most were
wrought by the labor of their hands, I said what industry and economy prevails here.

Masses of yarn were assorted to prepare stock-
ings for the father and brothers, and the fleece of
the lamb was sheared, and prepared for clothing,
in which they fearlessly braved the cold of winter.

The family were taught not to be ashamed of
honest industry, and it was a rule whatever was
done, to be done well. All seemed to obey, and
knew not how to forget this rule. There were sent
to market, in the best order, the surplus of the
dairy, and poultry yard, and loom. The mother
taught her daughters to consider the interest of
their father as their own, and instructed them by

her own example how to lessen his expenses. This seemed to me the kind of industry, which more than any other promoted cheerfulness and health.

The mother had no inclination to teach her daughters to be fine ladies, or to have them make a great appearance in the world; her constant aim was, to make them useful, and to prepare them for a future sphere of action.

Their countenances were pleasant and peaceful, like those who do right. Their quietness of mind seemed to proceed from a sense of justice, or of doing their duty even to inanimate things; for we owe a duty to every article in our possession, and to every utensil with which we work; the duty of keeping them in order, and in a good condition.

In reading we find that some of the most illustrious men that ever filled our country, were the sons of farmers. There industry was great to elevate those means, by which to accomplish the object in view. A sense of their industry alarmed them not. They were willing to labor, on account of studying the best means of relieving the world.

"In the country, we seem to stand in the midst of the great theatre of God's power and we feel an unusual proximity to our Creator. His blue and tranquil sky spreads itself over our heads, and we acknowledge the intrusion of no secondary agent in unfolding its vast expanse. Nothing but Omnipotence can work up the dark horrors of the tempest, dart the flashes of the lightning, and roll the long resounding murmur of the thunder.

How auspicious such a life to the noble sentiments of devotion! Besides, the situation of the

farmer is peculiarly favorable to purity and simplicity of moral sentiment. He is brought acquainted chiefly with the real and native wants of
mankind: employed solely in bringing food out of
the earth, he is not liable to be fascinated with the
fictitious pleasures, the unnatural wants, the fashionable follies and tyrannical vices, of more busy
and splendid life.

Still more favorable to the religious character of
the farmer is the circumstance, that, from the nature of rural pursuits, they do not so completely
engross the attention as other occupations. They
leave much time for contemplation, for reading,
and intellectual pleasures ; and these are peculiarly
grateful to the resident in the country.

Especially does the institution of the Sabbath
discover all its value to the tiller of the earth,
whose fatigue it solaces, whose hard labor it does
not interrupt, and who feels, on that day, the
worth of his moral nature, which cannot be understood by the busy man, who considers the repose of this day as interfering with his hopes of
gain, or professional employments. If, then, this
institution is of any moral and religious value, it
is to the country we must look for the continuance
of that respect and observance, which it merits."

I have often been led to contemplate the character of the farmers lot. He is the possessor of true
independence. His children are a part of his
wealth. If fortunate circumstances fail, they join
and help him, instead of burdening, and sinking him into deeper waters.

"Did man control his passions, and form his
conduct according to the dictates of wisdom, hu-

manity and virtue, the earth would no longer be desolated by cruelty; and human societies would live in order, harmony and peace. In those scenes of mischief and violence which fill the world, let man behold with shame, the picture of his vices, his ignorance and folly. Let him be humble by the mortifying view of his own perverseness ; but let not his ' heart fret against the Lord.' "

~~~~~~~~~~~~~~~~~~~~~~~~~~~~

LIFE IS SHORT.

THE village bell solemnly tolled. Numbers of people were seen slowly assembling at the funeral call. The hearse stood before the door of an ancient mansion, and seemed to be in readiness to bear some human soul.

As I passed, I made a stop. I heard the minister.lifting up his solemn voice in supplication that the living might be supported in willingness, in their bitter parting with the dead. I heard voices feebly mingling with his prayer. It was the voice of two orphan children, from whom their parents had been suddenly taken.

I followed with the mournful children to the graves of their parents. They saw their parents side by side, placed beneath the dark silent mansions of the tomb. Methought, as I saw the tears flow fast down their cheeks, that they said, "we have neither father or mother on earth." Then thought I, hush my dears, "God will be a father to the orphan."

The children returned, but in mental distress. Now no earthly hand to guide them, and no friend to their relief. The brother said, "I think of the loss of our parents." Then methought I heard a still small voice saying, "the righteous are rewarded in heaven." The sister arose from her knees, and seemed to bend calmly over the place from whence the dead had been taken. "Brother," said she, "I fancy the smile of our mother; who, amid her tears, was an expression all sublime."

With them, indeed, life was short. Ere a week had sunk into its sorrowing vision, the orphans were no more. The youth wasted; and his wild eye shrank at the glance and footstep of the stranger.

His sister companion repeated to him passages of Scripture, with which her memory was stored, and sang hymns, until she perceived that if he was in pain he complained not, if he might but hear her cheering voice. She made him more acquainted with the life of the compassionate Redeemer, how he left a blessing for those who should trust in him. And a voice from within, urged her never to desist from cherishing that tender and deep-rooted piety, because, like the flower of grass, he must soon pass away.

Seated upon his bed, she bowed her face to his to soothe and compose him. The dying youth pressed his sister to sing the hymn he loved. She controlled her grief to cheer him once more with its trembling harmony. "Sister," said he, "I should like to see my Uncle, before I resign my body into the arms of death." She answered, "I think, brother, that he will soon come." It was then that he breathed away his soul, whispering of the angels and their celestial melodies.

Gazing earnestly in his face, she saw the work of the destroyer. " Brother ! dear brother ! are you happy ?" " Sister," he replied, with a faint smile upon his ghastly features, " Christ's ready for me. I am willing to go to him." Tremulous tones, like those of a broken harp, rose above the grief, to comfort her dying brother. One sigh of icy breath was upon her cheek, as she joined it to his, one shudder and all was over.

Her Uncle entered thoughtlessly. She pointed to the cold immovable brow. "Behold," said she, "my brother ; see, he no longer suffers." She looked back to the fountains of other years, how that her happiness had been augmented by the presence of her brother, the sweet companion of her infancy. With tears, she committed her only seeming friend to the grave, beside her parents.

Ere another week closed, the sister was not among the living. In broken dreams, she fancied that she heard the voices of her parents, and her brother. She longed for an abode with the right-eous. She felt the utter necessity of deriving consolation, and the power of enduring her suf-ferings, wholly from above.

It was evident with beholders, that life with he was short. Her frame wasted ; and her deathly ountenance, told that life's abode was short. No friend to mingle in her prayers, and naught

to soothe her dying pillow. In silence, and unknown, she resigned herself into the arms of Jesus.

" Man that is born of woman, is of few days,
and full of trouble. He cometh forth like a flower,
and is cut down ; he fleeth also as a shadow, and
never continueth in one stay."

" I have seen a youth in the pride of his days ;
his cheeks glowed with beauty ; his limbs were
full of activity ; he leaped ; he walked ; he ran ;
he rejoiced in that he was more excellent than
those. I returned : he lay cold and stiff on the
bare ground ; his feet could no longer more, nor
his hands stretch themselves out ; his life was
departed from him ; and the breath out of his
nostrils. Therefore do I weep because DEATH is
in the world ; the spoiler is among the works of
God ; all that is made must be destroyed ; all that
is born must die." When I thought thereon, I
knew that life was short !"

DEATH OF THE CHRISTIAN.

THE Christian, and he alone, can triumph amidst
the agonies of dissolving nature, in a well groun-
ded hope of future felicity. There is a genuine
dignity in the death of the real believer. It is
not the vanity of an Augustus Cæsar, who called

his subjects around him; and after reminding them that he had lived in glory, bid them applaud him after death.

It is not the heroic stupidity of an Andre, who ostentatiously desired the spectators of his catastrophe, to witness that he died as a brave man. It is not the thoughtless courage of a professed hero, in the heat of spirits, and amidst the confusion of battles, rushing almost headlong upon certain destruction. It is not the hardy insensibility of an Indian warrior, exulting in the midst of surrounding flames, provoking his tormentors, and singing a merry song of death. He meanly retreats from evils, which Christian heroism would qualify to overcome by his exertions, or to endure with patience.

The votaries of fame may acquire a sort of insensibility to death and its consequences. But he alone whose peace is made with God, can walk with composure through the gloomy valley of the shadow of death, and fear no evil. Behold Chesterfield, after a life of pleasure, endeavoring to act the philosopher in death! But, alas! it proved fatal.

The man of intellectual genius may cause his wit to flash, and blaze, and burn; and as Pollock says of Byron, " He stands on the Alps — stands on the Appenines, and talks with thunder, as with friend to friend, and weave his garland from the lightning's flash in sportive twist," and then die, and is gone; but where?

A cultivated mind, and an unsanctified heart, may become one of the most awful scourges of this world. Such was Byron, such was Rosseau, and such was Voltaire, and many others.

On the other hand, behold the amiable, the virtuous, the pious Addison, in his dying scene. How humble, and at the same time, how dignified he appears.   His setting sun shone bright.   The evening of his life was pleasant and serene.   Observe him, ye admirers of fortitude ; view him in that critical hour, which emphatically tries men's souls ; and learn with what superior dignity of mind a Christian can die.

~~~~~~~~~~~~~~~~~~~~~~~~~~~~~~~~

REFLECTIONS UPON THE CLOSE OF LIFE.

WRITTEN ON VISITING THE GRAVE YARD AT NEW HAVEN, CT.

" WHEN we contemplate the close of life, the termination of man's designs and hopes ; the silence that now reigns among those who, a little while ago, were so busy or so gay ; who can avoid being touched with sensations at once awful and tender?   What heart but then warms with the glow of humanity ?   In whose eye does not the tear gather, on revolving the fate of passing short lived man ?"

The graves before me, and all around me, are thickly deposited.   The marble that speak the names, bid us prepare for DEATH.   How solemn is the thought that soon we, too, must lay low in the grave. The generations that now exist must pass away ; and more arise in their stead, to fill the places which they now occupy, and do effectual good.

Some of the marble speaks of those who have not long since died ; others appear quite ancient. Yet, memory can never fill the places of most of these, who slumber here in tombs. Trace back — their relations are not among the living. Ere a day they slumbered in the silent grave.

In the grave by my side sleeps some sainted priest ; the marble speaks his fame. Perhaps he has undergone the fatigues of life ; he has been an eminent servant in his Master's calling, and now has his reward in heaven. He has died the death of the righteous ; he has given up this world " with joy and not with grief." He has had different stations in life ; he has, perhaps, been in various parts of the world, has proclaimed the gospel to the heathen, he has experienced prosperity and adversity ; he has seen families and kindred rise and fall ; and he has now closed his eyes upon this world forever more.

Methinks I see before me the family burying ground. At the head sleeps the father and the mother. The children are deposited within the ground. The words about seem to say, live and die as did this family ; upon this saying I did relent.

As I walked on, I seated myself down upon a grave ; it was the grave of an infant. It seemed to be sleeping on until the resurrection " of both great and small." I said, before this day shall close, I too may sleep in death. Have I preserv.

ed that cheerful, and innocent countenance which this infant has shown? Then I prayed to the Lord to shelter me, and to deliver me from all evil.

I saw a countless number of trees. Among them was a willow. I thought of what a child once said. "Tree, why art thou always sad and drooping? Am I not kind unto thee? Do not the showers visit thee, and sink deep to refresh thy root? Hast thou sorrow at thy heart?" Then said an author — "but it answered not. And as it grew on, it drooped lower and lower; for it was a weeping willow."

I stooped myself down over the grave of an aged sire. I said to him, tell me of this grave! Methought that he answered — "ask him who rose again for me." Noble sire, thou hast seen peace and war succeeding in their turn; the face of thy country undergoing many alterations; and the very city in which thou dwelt, rising in a manner new around thee.

After all thou hast beheld, thine eyes are now closed forever. Thou wast becoming a stranger amidst a new succession of men. A race who knew thee not, had arisen to fill the earth. Thus passeth the world away; "and this great inn is by turns evacuated and replenished, by troops of succeeding pilgrims."

"O vain and inconstant world! O fleeting and transient life. When will the sons of men learn to think of thee as they ought? When will they learn humanity from the affliction of their brethren; or moderation and wisdom, from a sense of their own fugitive state?"

BIOGRAPHICAL.

LOUISA SEBURY.

Louisa Sebury was born at Hartford, Connecticut, March 12th, 1816. An ingenuous temper, a quickness of understanding, a benevolent spirit, a flexibility of nature, and a solemn sense of divine things, were observed in her tender age; and in the dangerous ascent of life, her feet were guided and preserved in the paths of rectitude and goodness; so that she was not only free from the stain of vice and vanity in her rising years, but looked to things superior to the world, and its vain and trifling amusements.

Her thirst for knowledge was great, although she had not the advantage which many have, who less improve it. But although not skilled in the depths of knowledge, yet she possessed Christian virtue, which often the profound historian does not.

In friendship, she was firm, affectionate, and

confiding. She rendered every service in her power to those whom she loved. She regarded all with whom she associated with Christian kindness, and by a warm and generous sympathy, she made their sorrows her own.

Though she was agreeable in her person, she did not sacrifice her time to the decoration of dress. She was always neat in her apparel, but did not allow the toilet to interfere with other duties. Her feelings were the kindest, and the most social; and her manners were unaffected. For empty ceremony and ostentious fashion, she had neither time nor taste.

All her deportment was marked by true humility. And though her excellence could not shield her from enmity, and from the slanders of that envy which follows eminent goodness, and "like the shadow, proves the substance true," she avoided resentment, and consided herself thus called upon to exercise the Christian virtue of forgiveness.

She was often a subject of ill health. Her last sickness was occasioned from a violent cold which she had taken. This terminated her existence. Now the value of that religion which she had chosen was fully realized. She was enabled to endure, without murmuring, severe affliction.

As religion was the subject of her meditations in health, it was more forcibly impressed upon her mind during illness. She knew the duty of resignation to the will of her Maker, and of dependence on the merits of a Redeemer. These sentiments were often expressed by her, to persons who visited her dying bed.

" A life so blameless, a trust so firm in God, a

mind so conversant with a future and better world, seemed to have divested death of terror. He came as a messenger to conduct her to that state of purity and bliss for which she had been preparing."

All future hopes of recovery, by her friends, were at length given over. To her it was not unwelcome news. Her parents mourned to think of the loss of so affectionate a daughter; great was her loss, seemingly, to her sisters; and society mourned the loss of a valuable friend.

Death to her was no unwelcome messenger. The close of her life was like the fading of a serene Sabbath into the holy quiet of its evening. The virtues which made her beloved, continued to flourish, and put forth new and fresh blossoms, until her life's end.

With so calm and peaceful a mind, so blessed and lively a hope, did this resigned friend of Christ wait for her Master's summons. It was on the 16th day of December, 1838, that her spirit departed. And methought I heard a voice saying, " Such shall hunger no more, neither thirst any more; for they have washed their robes, and made them white in the blood of the Lamb ?"

JULIA ANN PELL.

JULIA ANN PELL was born at Montville, Connecticut, in the year 1813.   She did not enjoy the privilege of living with her parents when a child. Her age did not exceed eight years, when she was sent to live with a family, where she served as an apprentice until she was eighteen.   From thence she went to East Granby and lived some years in the family of the Pastor of that village, where she was much respected for her honesty, and stability of character.

In the year of 1836, she thought to benefit herself by coming to Hartford : she therefore was obliged to leave the family, who much regretted her loss.

She remained in Hartford till the close of her life.   She was esteemed for good behavior, and assistance in society ; attending to the concerns of her own, and leaving alone those of others.   She did not figure in the gay and more fashionable forms of society, nor had she any particular relish for those external attractions, which wear such an alluring aspect to the fashionist and votary of worldly pleasure.

While young she had not the advantages of a school education.   Perhaps not attending school more than one or two days in a week.   Yet, even then, it was her most eager desire to be a scholar, though fortune seemed to forbid it.   She gained some of the rudiments of knowledge with great labor and difficulty; and her perseverance was put to a most severe trial.

The years of her childhood being spent in the country, she had less advantages of education than many. There being but one school, the scholars were quite numerous; and those whose station was inferior to many in the school, were neglected; their rights trampled upon, and their time abused.

She had a permanent regard for the Sabbath, and for religious services; attending both the Sabbath School, and divine worship three times upon that day. The intervals of worship, she spent in reading the Holy Scriptures, or religious books. She was exceedingly strict in her improvement of time. By rising early, she secured the best part of the day for her domestic employments, and for the necessary duties devolving upon her station. Simplicity of living and industrious habits, she particularly regarded; ornaments seldom known, among the nobility of a republic.

She took good care of all that was entrusted to her. Order she had practiced from a child, and she took delight in it. "A place for every thing and every thing in its place," was one of her characteristics. Said she, "a constant habit of putting the same things in the same places, and performing the same duties at the same times, will always enable us to find what we want, and to do what is to be done, readily, pleasantly, and without any annoyance to others."

In the year of 1838, she became a member of the Church of Christ. The society of religious

5

persons was very pleasant and agreeable to her; and to the end of her days she was anxious to live in the fear of God, and to walk before him with a humble heart.

Her last sickness, which terminated in death, was painful in the extreme. She bore it with Christian patience. When physicians and friends had hopes of her recovery, said she, "I shall never recover." Under all trying circumstances, she enjoyed the sweet peace of the believer, founded on the Christian hope.

When she had the smallest prospect of life, she seemed far from being alarmed with the view of her dissolution. She expressed her willingness either to live or die, as it should please Divine Providence. "If," said she, "I had any hopes of recovery, it would be my soul's desire to bring glory to the name of the Lord, proportionable to all the dishonor I have done Him, in my whole life: and particularly by endeavors to convince others of the danger of their condition, if they continue impenitent; and by telling them how graciously God has dealt with me."

All the faculties of her mind were perfect until the last. It is thought that few people see death approach them, as she did. In short, her death was like her life; easy, unaffected, and pious.

The morning that she died, she came down stairs with little help, and appeared to be gaining health. But such appearances are often deceptive. She sat down awhile, when she was persuaded to return to her room; she seemed to be unwilling, and said that she would like to sit awhile. She had grown weaker by leaving her room, and required much help to get back. When she reached her room, she threw herself upon her bed and exclaimed, " Never again shall I see, what I have seen."

Between six and seven in the evening, a friend went to her room, and said that she was going to hear a lecture on that evening. She expressed her willingness, and wished to have her repeat to her what she heard when she returned. The friend had not been long seated before some one called for her. Said she, " Is Julia dead ?" It was indeed true. She had ceased to breathe. Thus she peacefully died, in the 27th year of her age, March 17th, 1839.

ELIZA LOOMIS SHERMAN.

ELIZA LOOMIS SHERMAN was born at Hartford, Conn., December, in the year 1822. She was the daughter of Henry Sherman, and enjoyed the benefit of the example of pious parents. She early displayed an amiable disposition, a mind of strong powers, and an affectionate heart.

The subject of this sketch, from a child, never enjoyed good health ; but was always feeble and inclined to disease. She was ever pale, and looked like one that was smitten in youth, and was declining every day.

While small, she was not like most chlidren which many have seen ; she was diligent and thoughtful, and always seemed to take an interest in the God of creation ; she was never quick or unsubmissive, but always bore the same composed and pleasant countenance.

Though not having the advantage of many children, on account of her health, yet, while at the last school she attended, and at others before, she gained a common school education. But it is probable, had she had the advantage which many have, she might have been more learned. But the time which health permitted her to attend was very irregular.

Her moral sensibilities were uniformly strong. To do right, to avoid wounding the feelings of others, and always to speak the truth, were her rules of action. Her conscience was tender, and if she had committed any fault, she acknowledged it with frankness.

She was a favorite with her teachers. They were gratified by her proficiency, and pleased with her amiable disposition. She realized the importance of a good education, and while persevering, reaped the reward, prepared for every faithful scholar, increase in knowledge and habits of self-control.

When quite young her excellent father died, and she, with a younger sister, was then under the care of a tender and pious mother. In the winter of 1838, she made a public profession of her Christian faith. In this act, she always rejoiced, as giving strength to the confidence which, from still earlier years, she had placed in her heavenly protector. She now sought the society of the wise and pious, as she had ever been wont to do, that of those who were older than herself.

At the age of fifteen, she was capable of superintending her mother's largest tables ; if she saw any thing go on wrong among the servants, she would forbear mentioning it to them, until she had first spoken to her mother. She would say, " I would rather you would speak to them, for I am younger than they are." So would this young person try to keep friends among all individuals.

All who knew her, spoke of her being singular from most persons of her age. She was an example for all who did, and do not put their trust in a crucified Saviour.

In the winter of 1839, her health began visibly to decline. Symptoms of pulmonary consumption were plainly revealed. She employed physicians from several places ; but help for her was now given over. And had she wished for shelter beneath a Georgian clime, that privilege would not have been granted her; on account of the laws.

The following spring disease become seated. She was no more to go among her friends, or to behold her school room. Her frame wasted to a skeleton, and a hollow, racking cough, told that she was soon to die.

Said a friend, " I called upon her one day, I found her reclining upon the sofa, her head resting upon the side ; she exhibited great difficulty in breathing, but seemed calm and serene, trusting

in God, who had been with her through affliction."
She lived a life of prayer. The Bible which
she had loved and obeyed, was her stay, as she
passed through the dark valley. Like a child
yielding to its parents, she laid herself in His everlasting arms.

The lovely works of God were then brighter to
her than they ever yet had been; the precious
truths from the Bible, which from earliest memory
she had loved, tarried with her, till the Angels
came.

It was in the evening, month of August, 1839,
that death came upon her like a friend, soothing
her into gentle slumber. Without a gasp or strug-
gle she slept in Jesus, "patience having had its
perfect work."

Let the young, in forming their own characters,
be assiduous to secure the same sources of happiness, which cheered this lovely and exemplary
young lady, and enabled her, during long decline,
to comfort others with her own radiant countenance, and to close her life like a music strain.

The pleasing contemplation of so peaceful and
happy a conclusion of life as this, and others
which we often read, is sufficient, to elevate the
soul, and to make all the glories and enjoyments
of this transient scene sink into nothing. Ah!
these are favored, precious moments, when the
divine power of religion breaks in upon us, dissolves
the enchantment of the world, dissipates the mist
of vain doubts and speculation, and raises a fer-
vent aspiration, that whatever may be our allotment
through life, we may die the death of the righteous, and the love of God be our portion for ever!

ELIZABETH LOW,

ELIZABETH Low was born in Cooperstown, New York, June 10th, 1818. She appeared to possess a truly noble mind, an amiable and benevolent temper. Her pious resignation, and religious deportment, under the pressure of very deep distress, afford a highly instructive example, and an eminent instance of the glory of religion to sustain the mind, in the greatest storms and dangers, when the waves of affliction threaten to overwhelm it.

This young lady spent a great part of her time in perusing the Holy Scriptures, and other religious books. She had a just esteem for all persons whom she thought religious and virtuous. She appeared to be happily disposed from very early life, being good and gentle before she was capable of knowing that it was her duty to be so. This temper continued with her, through the whole course of her life.

At the age of fourteen, she made a public profession of her Christian faith. Whatever her other virtues, their lustre was greatly increased by her humility. She was strict in the observance of religion. She adopted the rule of the Psalmist, "evening, morning and noon, will I pray," and retired three times a day for secret prayer.

But her health which had always been feeble, began to decline. Consumption was deeply seated.

At times she was able to leave her room, and would attend a benevolent institution. From thence she took a piece of work, and endeavored to finish it; but it seemed as though her health would not permit. She had such a desire to finish it, that she would seek her bed for rest, and then rise and go to her work. At length she finished it, and sent it to the Society.

She was at last confined to her room, no more to go out of it. She was visited by many pious persons, to whom she expressed a desire and willingness to die; to depart from this world of sorrow, to be with her God. The whole time of her sickness, she was in a cheerful, thankful frame of mind; leaving all to God, and referring to the disposal of Providence.

She was continually blessing those around her, as death approached. " May we meet in an eternal, a glorious world! Beseeching them to press forward, for a glorious prize awaited them; to be faithful unto death and they should obtain it."

She expressed a wish to a female friend to have her present, when she should breathe her last. When the time approached, she said to her mother, " send for this dear friend, that she may witness my death." Ere that friend reached her, she had fallen asleep in the arms of her Saviour.

A short time before she died, she said to this friend, " I have an article of dress in such a place, which will answer for my SHROUD. If you will have the goodness to prepare my grave clothes, and have them in readiness, that I may see them before I die, you will be rewarded, and I receive satisfaction."

According to her wish, those garments were prepared, and brought to her room. The friend told her mother, that she need not show them to her unless she called for them. She did not however call for them, until this friend arrived. At length she called for them; they were shown to her. A benignant lustre enkindled in her dim eyes, while surveying the robes, which, at her own request, had been prepared to deck her for the tomb!

At one instant, she found death stealing upon her; a little while after, and she would be singing that sweet song,—"Blessing, and honor, and glory, and power, be unto Him that sitteth upon the throne, and to the Lamb for ever and ever!" She made a request to see all her dear friends around her bedside.

She mentioned the names of those, whom she thought would take the most interest in witnessing her death. They were sent for; all of them came except one; he being a minister of the Gospel, was out of town. As soon as they gathered around her, she said that one was absent. On being told the cause, she appeared satisfied.

Thus she lived, and thus she died. An eminant instance of Christain fortitude, patience, and meekness. Thus was she prepared to say, "Oh! death, where is thy sting! Oh! grave, where is thy victory!" It was on the 15th of September, 1838, that her spirit departed, to become an inhabitant of those regions above, where just spirits reign.

POETRY.

ADVICE TO YOUNG LADIES.

Day after day I sit and write,
　　And thus the moments spend —
The thought that occupies my mind, —
　　Compose to please my friend.

And then I think I will compose,
　　And thus myself engage —
To try to please young ladies minds,
　　Which are about my age.

The greatest word that I can say, —
　　I think to please, will be,
To try and get your learning young,
　　And write it back to me.

But this is not the only thing
　　That I can recommend ;
Religion is most needful for
　　To make in us a friend.

At thirteen years I found a hope,
　　And did embrace the Lord ;
And since, I've found a blessing great,
　　Within his holy word.

Perchance that we may ne'er fulfill,
　　The place of aged sires,
But may it with God's holy will,
　　Be ever our desires.

LINES,

WRITTEN UPON BEING EXAMINED IN SCHOOL STUDIES FOR THE PREPARATION OF A TEACHER.

Teach me, O! Lord, the secret errors of my way,
Teach me the paths wherein I go astray,
Learn me the way to teach the word of love,
For that's the pure intelligence above.
As well as learning, give me that truth forever—
Which a mere worldly tie can never sever,
For though our bodies die, our souls will live
    forever.
To cultivate in every youthful mind,
Habitual grace, and sentiments refined.
Thus while I strive to govern human heart,
May I the heavenly precepts still impart;
Oh! may each youthful bosom, catch the sacred
    fire,
And youthful mind to virtues throne aspire.
Now fifteen years their destined course have run,
In fast succession round the central sun;
How did the follies of that period pass,
I ask myself—are they inscribed in brass!
Oh! Recollection, speed their fresh return,
And sure 'tis mine to be ashamed and mourn.
"What shall I ask, or what refrain to say?
Where shall I point, or how conclude my lay?
So much my weakness needs—so oft thy voice,
Assures that weakness, and confirms my choice.
Oh, grant me active days of peace and truth,
Strength to my heart, and wisdom to my youth,
A sphere of usefulness—a soul to fill
That sphere with duty, and perform thy will."

REFLECTIONS,

WRITTEN ON VISITING THE GRAVE OF A VENERATED FRIEND.

DEEP in this grave her bones remain,
She's sleeping on, bereft of pain,
Her tongue in silence now does sleep,
And she no more time's call can greet.

She liv'd as all God's saints should do,
Resign'd to death and suffering too ;
She feels not pain or sin oppress,
Nor does of worldly cares possess.

White were the locks that thinly shed
Their snows around her honor'd head,
And furrows not to be effac'd
Had age amid her features trac'd.

I said, my sister, DO tread light,
Faint as the stars that gleam at night,
Nor pluck the tender leaves that wave
In sweetness over this sainted grave.

The rose I've planted by her side,
It tells me of that fate decri'd ;
And bids us all prepare to die,
For that our doom is hast'ning nigh.

Oh ! that the gale that sweeps the heath,
Too roughly o'er your leaves should breathe,
Then sigh for her—and when you bloom
Scatter your fragrance o'er her tomb.

Alone I've wander'd through the gloom,
To pour my lays upon her tomb;
And I have mourn'd to see her bed
With brambles and with thorns o'erspread.

O, surely, round her place of rest
I will not let the weed be blest,
It is not meet that she should be
Forgotten or unblest by me.

My sister said, " tell of this grave!"
Go ask, said I, the thoughtless wave;
And spend one hour in anxious care—
In duty, penitence, and prayer.

Farewell! let memory bestow,
That all may soon be laid as low,
For out of dust, God did compose,
We turn to dust, to sleep, repose.

I HAVE NO BROTHER.

I HAVE no Brother! for he died
    When I was very young;
But still his memory round my heart
    Like morning mists has hung.

They tell me of his infant form,
　　With whom I often played;
And of a soft and gentle hand,
　　Our youthful thoughts had weigh'd.

The image of my Henry dear,
　　A sister has wept below;
Art thou with Christ, the sinners friend;
　　Dost thou of Heaven then know?"

My young companion in the dust,
　　My one—my morning friend;
The youthful one I lov'd at first—
　　The last o'er whom I bend.

But soon that little flower must rise,
　　Its light must then be known:
Lo! thence its spirit sought the sky—
　　The sister mourn'd alone.

Short, like thine, some transient date,
　　They drink the morning breath,
Yet, my brother, thou must sleep,
　　Thy spirit sank—in death.

Brother! thou wast my only one,
　　Belov'd from childhood's years,
A sweet companion of my youth,
　　How doleful it appears!

Alas! he died; oh, grief restrain—
　　The silent anguish of the mind;
Intrinsic love these lines do prompt,
　　Revive my spirits, be resign'd.

6

ON THE DISMISSION OF A SCHOOL TERM.

Ah, children dear, the hour draws near,
The sentence speeds — to part, to part ;
Come try and treasure in each heart,
Instructions of superior worth ,
What we have gain'd the winter past,
O, let it not be lost at last,
And let it not be turned to mirth.

Guide thou their steps to endless love, and bliss,
Rule thou in peace their Father. And in this,
Forgive in us, whate'er has been amiss.

Improve your privileges while you stay,
Ye pupils ; so that on that great day,
Humbly may have to say,
Judge Father ! For in thee we trust,
Christ our Saviour deign'd to die,
And we believe — we altogether must :
And thus conclude my lay.

THE TRUE FRIEND.

YOUNG persons, it is true, admire
The heart that burns with ardent fire —
　　Where comes no sob or sigh,
They bear the summer's heat in measure,
If they enjoy it all with pleasure,
　　Fatigue and trouble fly.

She is precisely like yourself —
In habits, principles, and wealth,
　　In beauty's opening prime ;
Her eyes and voice are of the same,
And like you is array'd in name,
　　Useful alike in time.

Our dearest friends on earth do die,
We mourn disconsolate — and why !
　　Their bodies are at rest !
But now the friend of whom I speak,
Is one whom all of you should seek,
　　This friend is really best.

In language beautiful, might she
From Ruth and Time address thee ;
　　"With thee, I ever go,
Where thou diest, I will die,
Where thou art buried I will lie ;
　　Lord deal with me thus so."

An introduction to this friend,
So surely ought you to attend,

Strive daily to improve ;
Are you industrious, pious, good ?
If true — the same is understood —
   By friendship ne'er to move.

If you persist in wrongful deeds,
She has a way in which she heeds ;
   The heart has weight of stone :
'Tis said by some a punishment,
Severe to wrongful sentiment,
   The feelings never won.

Be punctual to appointed time,
Frank to the questions that are mine,
   Agree as I propose :
Set down at slumber, wait for me,
And answer what I say to thee,
   And unto me disclose !

She, several questions you will ask,
Happy if you say yes, in task,
   This Friend most true in heart ;
That gold most pure, that rust cannot,
That thief nor robber, can't corrupt,
   This Friend is ne'er to part.

MEMORY OF MARY.

Sleep on, dearest, take thy rest,
  Address thy dreamless bed,
Thou art surely now more blest,
  Then any worldly head.

Thou wast simple in thy day,
  Quiet in thy death,
And ere enur'd to childish play,
  Yet now in ceasing breath.

" Suffer children unto me,"
  Is what our Saviour said ;
Oh ! how delightful that must be,
  How blest the early dead !

Ere sin might wound thy tender breast,
  Or sorrow cause a tear,
Rise to thy home of sacred rest,
  In yon celestial sphere.

Thy daughter kneels before the throne ;
  Ah, mother shed no tear,
Give up, nor do in sorrow mourn,
  Remember God is near.

Parents ne'er wish thy Mary hence,
  She was as only lent,
Oh ! *never* wish her back from thence,
  Strive to be confident.

When the arc-angel's trump shall blow,
　　And souls to bodies join,
Millions will wish their lives below,
　　Had been as short as thine !

~~~~~~~~~~~~~~~~~~

THE INFANT CLASS.

WRITTEN IN SCHOOL.

THIS, my youngest class in school,
　　Is what I do admire ;
Their sweetest, ever perfect praise,
　　Their eyes as sparkling fire.

How oft I've blessed them in my heart,
　　Besuoght that every grace
And consolation, might there dwell,
　　To cheer each youthful face.

I love them all as children each,
　　How happy they appear :
O, may no dull unclouded path,
　　Make happiness to fear.

How sweet their prayerful voices join,
　　To say what I do teach :
Their infant voices, how adorn'd,
　　How full of music each.

When out of school, how oft I think
Of these, my little ones,
But when in school, how glances all,
They shine like many suns.

They gather round me, one by one,
Like darlings to be taught ;
Ah, there behold my orphan dear,
For me she now has sought.

Dearest, we soon must say farewell,
May God your steps approve,
If then on earth we no more meet,
Or nev'er do this course more greet,
May we in Christ e'er move.

THE RESIDENCE OF MY FATHER.

How pleasantly my home does stand,
The scenery round is all but grand,
The noise is lull'd by rippling stream,
There all the rays of sun-shine gleam.

Thence at the foot of some lone tree,
Lull'd by the hum of wandering bee,
Or lisping to the whispering wind,
Proves satisfaction for the mind.

The morning lays are birds in song,
So often o'er the house they throng;
They perch upon the loftiest trees,
Where hum some very busy bees.

Delightful garden ; now art thou
Among the beauties shining now :
The flowers are now in vareid bloom,
They shine as does the sun at noon,
The moss-cup, and perennial flowers,
Are too, refresh'd by genial showers.

You rest, meek plants, nor do intrude,
Or trouble this deep solitude ;
Behold the vines that twine the bowers,
Adorn'd with decorating flowers,
Observe the violet modest blue,
It is a ever changeless hue,
The snow-drop and the lilly white,
Are ting'd with meekness ever bright.

Heaven bless you, O ye *groves*,
Of which my father knows,
I thank you to ye sounding stream,
How oft you've woke the musing dream,
And blent thine echo with my thought,
How oft I've thank'd thee for thy draught.

I soon may bid you all adieu,
For we cannot always stay,
And meet a scenery quite anew ;
I'm sure to leave it, may be true,
And then we hasten and away :
Then may this Eden, beauty be
The same to stranger as to me.

THE INQUIRY.

" Why art thou dull and dreary" ?
   I ask'd a lonely man,
Why is thy look thus sad ?
   Thy countenance thus wan ?
Do you for country pine ?
   Does care now wound your breast?
Are you with grief oppress'd ?
   Of friends and hope bereft ?

Does memory love to linger
   With bright and joyous hours,
That brings a gleam of happiness,
   Ere life around you lowers ?
And think a dream all useful
   That lingers round the past ;
And brings bright images to view,
   Of joys that cannot last ?

Are you remote from home,
   Upon a stranger shore ?
A suffering son of Italy ?
   And delt with as of yore ?
Have you upon the battle field,
   Beheld your brothers' cries ?
Ah ! then upon the slaughter'd land,
   Behold him, — there he dies !

He paused, and solemnly did he
   Upturn his holy eyes ;

Thou hast not had one solemn thought;
   I mourn for kindred skies.
I mourn for sin and death alone,
   It does my frame oppress.
I think of all the heavenly joys,
   Although I can't possess.

From thence, I turn'd about to think,
   And overwhelme'd in grief,
I felt the heavy load oppress.
   O! speed me quick relief!

FORGET ME NOT.

When in the morning's misty hour,
When the sun beems gently o'er each flower;
When thou dost cease to smile benign,
And think each heart responds with thine,
When seeking rest among divine,
               Forget me not.

When the last rays of twilight fall,
And thou art pacing yonder hall;
When mists are gathering on the hill,
Nor sound is heard save mountain rill,
When all around bids peace be still,
               Forget me not.

When the first star with brilliance bright,
Gleams lonely o'er the arch of night;
When the bright moon dispels the gloom,
And various are the stars that bloom,
And brighten as the sun at noon,
                    Forget me not.

When solemn sighs the hollow wind,
And deepen'd thought enraps the mind;
If e'er thou doest in mournful tone,
E'er sigh because thou feel alone,
Or wrapt in melancholy prone,
                    Forget me not.

When bird does wait thy absence long,
Nor tend unto its morning song;
While thou art searching stoic page,
Or listening to an ancient sage,
Whose spirit curbs a mournful rage,
                    Forget me not.

Then when in silence thou doest walk,
Nor being round with whom to talk;
When thou art on the mighty deep,
And do in quiet action sleep;
If we no more on earth do meet,
                    Forget me not.

When brightness round thee long shall bloom,
And knelt remembering those in gloom;
And when in deep oblivion's shade,
This breathless, mouldering form is laid,
And thy terrestrial body staid,
                    Forget me not.

" Should sorrow cloud thy coming years,
And bathe thy happiness in tears,
Remember, though we're doom'd to part,
There lives one fond and faithful heart,
      That will forget thee not."

MEMORY OF GUSTEEN.

How blest thy infant daughter now,
  How sweet is her repose ;
Before Almighty God does bow,
  Forever — and no close.

Thy infant is a seraph now,
  Parents shed thou no tear ;
But then in God do thou
  E'er trust, — and like him do appear.

Thy beauteous smile was ever fair,
  Thy lip and eye was bright,
Thy mother mourn'd the ceasing care,
  Which was to her delight.

A fairer babe there hast not been,
  Clung to its mother's breast ;
But with thee then decease was seen,
  It ceas'd, — and thou didst rest.

Then parents count her death no loss,
　　But rather count it gain ;
Nor do with looks of sore remorse,
　　Ever wish her back again.

Then at the last — the judgment day,
　　Thy infant dear shall rise,
And heavenly scenes to her portray,
　　Her home — the heavenly skies.

Then at that solemn, trying hour,
　　The wicked oft will say,
O ! that divine almighty power,
　　Would send a heavenly ray.

ALONE I'VE WANDERED.

AFAR alone I've wander'd,
　　Brisk at the evening tide ;
Where no footsteps were heard,
　　Where fate was not decried.

Alone, I love to wander,
　　Slow musing by my way,
And think of God's creation,
　　And the weary man astray.

Before the sun-shine sinks,
   I bend my way from home,
To admire the works of nature;
   And thus I like to roam.

The verdant lawn seems dazzling;
   I smell the scent of flowers.
How precious are those moments,
   Delightful, are those hours.

I look up to the heavens,
   Behold each solemn star;
Their glittering light allures me —
   How beautiful they are!

Then God who made all worlds,
   At the last solemn day,
Unto righteous men will say, —
   Ye join the heavenly lay.

THE NATIVES OF AMERICA.

TELL me a story, father please,
And then I sat upon his knees.
Then answer'd he, — "what speech make known,
Or tell the words of native tone,
Of how my Indian fathers dwelt,
And, of sore oppression felt;
And how they mourned a land serene,
It was an ever mournful theme."

Yes, I replied, — I like to hear,
And bring my father's spirit near;
Of every pain they did forego,
Oh, please to tell me all you know.
In history often I do read,
Of pain which none but they did heed.

He thusb egan.   " We were a happy race,
When we no tongue but ours did trace,
We were in ever peace,
We sold, we did release —
Our brethren, far remote, and far unknown,
And spake to them in silent, tender tone.
We all were then as in one band,
We join'd and took each others hand;
Our dress was suited to the clime,
Our food was such as roam'd that time,
Our houses were of sticks compos'd;
No matter, — for they us enclos'd.

But then discover'd was this land indeed
By European men; who then had need
Of this far country.   Columbus came afar,
And thus before we could say Ah !
What meaneth this ? — we fell in cruel hands.
Though some were kind, yet others then held bands
Of cruel oppression. Then too, foretold our chief,—
Beggars you will become — is my belief.
We sold, then some bought lands,
We altogether moved in foreign hands.

Wars ensued.   They knew the handling of fire-
    arms.
Mothers spoke, — no fear this breast alarms,

They will not cruelly us oppress,
Or thus our lands possess.
Alas! it was a cruel day; we were crush'd:
Into the dark, dark woods we rush'd
To seek a refuge.

My daughter, we are now diminish'd, unknown,
Unfelt! Alas! no tender tone
To cheer us when the hunt is done;
Fathers sleep, — we're silent every one.

Oh! silent the horror, and fierce the fight,
When my brothers were shrouded in night;
Strangers did us invade — strangers destroy'd
The fields, which were by us enjoy'd.

Our country is cultur'd, and looks all sublime,
Our fathers are sleeping who lived in the time
That I tell. Oh! could I tell them my grief
In its flow, that in roaming, we find no relief.

I love my country; and shall, until death
Shall cease my breath.

Now daughter dear I've done,
Seal this upon thy memory; until the morrow's sun
Shall sink, to rise no more;
And if my years should score,
Remember this, though I tell no more."

CHRIST'S DEPARTED.

CHRIST'S departed are at rest,
  Their souls are free from care,
Their last abode is with the blest;
  NONE BUT THE BLEST are there.

They thought not of the world at large,
  But trusting in their God;
They learn'd their duty to discharge,
  On earth's yet dreary sod.

They trusted in the Lord above,
  Commended him their frame,
Thought on a Saviour's dying love,
  And cherish'd long his name.

Such spirits hence, shall never mourn,
  Or wailing tears be shed;
But firmer in their trust be borne,
  To glories far ahead.

They wake no more with greeting smile,
  Gay voice or buoyant tread;
And yet some voices say the while,
  Of sleepers, — they are dead.

The bless'd in Christ, 'tis true do sleep
  They sleep, but are not dead;
Angels around their beds do keep,
  They lightly, softly tread.

Like theirs — our transient date must come,
    How soon we cannot tell ;
But if in God we trust like some,
    Henceforth, forever well.

TO THE FIRST OF AUGUST.

Britannia's isles proclaim,
    That freedom is their theme ;
And we do view those honor'd lands,
    With soul-delighting mien.

And unto those they held in gloom,
    Gave ev'ry one their right ;
They did disdain fell slavery's shade,
    And trust in freedom's light.

Then unto ev'ry British blood,
    Their noble worth revere,
And think them ever noble men,
    And like them, hence appear.

And when on Britain's isles remote,
    We're then in freedom's bounds,
And while we stand on British ground,
    You're free, — you're free, — resounds.

Lift ye that country's banner high,
   And may it nobly wave,
Until beneath the azure sky,
   Man shall be no more a slave.

And oh ! when youth's extatic hour,
   When winds and torrents foam,
And passion's glowing noon are past,
   To bless that free born home ;

Then let us celebrate the day,
   And lay the thought to heart,
And teach the rising race the way,
   That they may not depart.

A MOTHER TO HER FATHERLESS SON.

It was a mother, who at eve,
In thought so holy did believe ;
Who sat within an ancient dome,
That once had been her favor d home.

The father slept in vaulted walls,
He who had own'd those graceful halls ;
And o'er his grave a marble stone,
Proclaimed his earthly grandeur gone.

And 'mid the eve the mother came,
And call'd aloud her son's bright name,
"Come unto me my own dear son,
Thou art to me an only one."

Then came the beauteous boy so bright,
And then methought, you do love right,
And sat beside her, who had been
His guide through life, through faith unseen.

My son, — the faithful mother said,
Your sire is sleeping 'mid the dead ;
Remember though on earth we part,
That we must give to God our heart.

Although of royal men was he,
The greatest of them all to be ;
Still he was of a spirit meek,
It teaches you his place to seek.

Attend to all my son I say,
And do the Bible's gems display ;
This book will teach you wisdom all,
And how the first of us did fall.

Improve your ever precious time,
Listen to Homer's page sublime,
Attend to Cicero's words so strong,
Ere long complete a Virgil's song.

And when afar from me you're moved,
I oft shall think, — how much improved ?
If you your father's talent bear,
Thou art prepared for worldly care.

You have as great a chance to be,
As good, as wise, as lov'd as he ;
'Mid darkness and amid dismay,
He went rejoicing on his way.

My son, — thou bear'st his noble name,
Behold those walls, their stately fame,
The hand that used to lead you there,
Is sleeping silently, — oh ! where !

Thy father sleeps in yonder tomb,
Forever is shaded by the gloom ;
Possess his blood within thy veins,
And more than THIS for thee remains.

This world shall try thee o'er my son,
Thou ever dear, — thou lovely one ;
Prepare to meet a worldly foe,
May God be with thee when you go !

DAUGHTER'S INQUIRY.

I ASKED if father 's to return,
  He left some years ago,
And I have never seen him since, —
  That all sad parting blow.

l said, my father, if you please
     Do guide the ship no more,
Some other can your place fulfill,
     And others can explore.

If not, dear father, do resign
     This ever roaming life,
Oh, do not spend your life in this,
     An ever mournful strife.

Perchance that you may ne'er return,
     The billows thence your grave,
O'er which no storied wind shall rise,
     No music but the wave.

Thus you have roam'd the southern seas,
     And riches with you flow ;
You have beheld the bread fruit tree,
     The yam and millet grow.

You've been around the world again,
     And view'd it o'er and o'er ;
Then why do you thus wish to go,
     And speed the parting hour ?

I never may behold you more,
     Or seek advice so dear ;
Oh ! how can I to strangers tell,
     Or trust a feeling near.

Some say there's danger on the sea,
     No more than on the land ;
I think we're liable to this,
     On sea, or desert sand.

I begged him, father do not go,
  For when you left me last,
You said you would not go again :
  My childish joys are past.

Then speed the long farewell ;
  You must depart in haste,
The seamen are on board her decks,
  To plough the billow's waste.

He knelt, and pray'd of God above,
  My dearest daughter spare ;
If not on earth, in heaven to meet,
  Sure trusting in Thy care.

And oft I sit me down, and think
  My father's absence long ;
I wonder if he will return,
  To bless my childish song.

Some say, "he must be dead, I think,
  Or we should from him hear ;"
Sometimes I think it must be true,
  And shed a mournful tear.

If then he is on distant shores,
  May God his steps approve,
And find a rest in heaven at last,
  And then with Christ to move.

THE GRAVE.

WHO sleeps in silence 'neath this mound?
   Whose dust does here repose?
Is it unholy, sinful ground, —
   And blood upon the rose?

Does there a hero sleep beneath?
   Some chief of spotless fame?
The flowrets here no fragrance breathe,
   No marble speaks his name!

Does an historian's wither'd form,
   Here lie so dark and low?
I hear no requiem but the storm,
   No mournful sound of wo.

Is it a humble, Christian child,
   Who free from care lies here?
Around this spot, thus drear and wild —
   And not one friendly tear!

No, — the dust that moulders here enshrin'd,
   Was here an infant heart, —
A wreath by beauty's hand entwin'd
   Did love to it impart.

The parents wept about its grave,
   And friends its loss did mourn;
But tears could not their darling save,
   It died, — they thought it wrong.

AUTHOR'S FAREWELL.

FAREWELL my reader, I must close,
Yet I feel anxious to compose
As much again, if I could find
Words all important for the mind.

Some time before I dare begin, —
A work commencing with my pen,
But stiil encourag'd by each friend,
I hope the time to rightly spend.

It does become us all full well —
To act the part that will excel,
And keep each precept in our heart,
That never ought, but may depart.

Our days pass on — a fleeting year,
Once more has swept our broad career ;
What if our tongues in silence sleep,
And we no more time's call can greet !

Oh ! let the soul her slumber break,
Let thought be quicken'd and awake —
How soon this life is passed and gone,
And death comes softly stealing on.

Swiftly our pleasures glide away,
Our hearts recall the distant day,
The moments that are speeding fast,
We heed not — but the past — the past.

Death is most sure for all mankind,
It's what our Father had design'd ;
He has prepared all future time,
And He can say, — all nature's mine.

Grant that we each trust in the Lord,
And ne'er forget His holy word ;
It is all wise, the better book,
And all who care will in it look.

Then shall our glories rise, and fair,
Nor spot, nor stain, nor wrinkle bear,
Then shall we reach our Saviour's home —
And never, never, more to roam.

Oh ! deep the horror, fierce the sound,
A voice from its sepulchral ground, —
Says,—" I am the grave, the still dark womb,
Where mortals all must find a tomb."